936·3

HISTORIC SCOTLAND

VIKING

SCOTLAND

CIRCENC
WITI

D1346845

cirencester
college
a beacon college

HISTORIC ■ SCOTLAND

VIKING SCOTLAND

ANNA RITCHIE

B. T. Batsford Ltd/Historic Scotland

For my mother, who shares my curiosity about the past.

© Anna Ritchie 1993

First published 1993
Reprinted 1994

Typeset by Servis Filmsetting Ltd
and printed in Great Britain by
The Bath Press, Bath

Published by B T Batsford Ltd
4 Fitzhardinge Street, London W1H 0AH

A CIP catalogue record for this book is available from
the British Library

ISBN 0 7134 7225 1 (cased)
       0 7134 7316 9 (limp)

Contents

Illustrations

Colour plates

Acknowledgements

There have been several important excavations of Viking Age and late Norse sites in recent years, not all of which are published yet, and I am indebted to many colleagues for help and information. In particular, I should like to thank Colleen Batey, James Barrett, Robert Beck, Gerald Bigelow, Anne Brundle, Trevor Cowie, Barbara Crawford, Magnar Dalland, Alison Fraser, Peter Hill, John Hunter, Olwyn Owen, Christopher Morris, Alison Sheridan and Val Turner.

I am very grateful to my father-in-law, W.F. Ritchie, and to my Batsford editor, Sarah Vernon-Hunt, who between them greatly improved the style and readability of the text. I should also like to thank David Breeze and Graham Ritchie for their helpful comments on the text, and Alan Braby who created the reconstruction drawings as well as drawing most of the other line illustrations. I am grateful to Peter Kemmis Betty of Batsford for his patient encouragement.

I am indebted to the following individuals and institutions for photographs, for which they own the copyright unless stated: David Breeze (**102, 121**), Dennis Coutts (**110, colour plate 12**), Barbara and Robert Crawford (**3, 104**), Tom Gray (**83**), John Hunter and the University of Bradford (**10, 28**), The Orkney Library (**117, 118**), Christopher D. Morris (**107**), Graham Ritchie (**colour plates 1, 5, 7, 10**), Crown Copyright: Royal Commission on the Ancient and Historical Monuments of Scotland (**6, 11, 13, 45, 62, 67–70, 73–81, 97–8, 120–1, colour plates 3, 6**), Trustees of the National Museums of Scotland (**8, 17–18, 26, 29–31, 46, 57–60, 63–6, 71, 92–3, colour plate 4**), The Whithorn Trust (**85, 87**). All the remaining illustrations are Crown Copyright: Historic Scotland.

CHAPTER ONE

Atlantic Scotland and the Viking adventure

If you walk through the streets of Kirkwall or Lerwick today, you are conscious at every turn of their Viking past, from the names of streets to the goods on sale: St Olaf's Wynd, for instance, or a sweater hand-knitted with Norse runes. This is more than a response to a tourist industry hungry for the romance of Viking longships. Orkney and Shetland became thoroughly Scandinavian during six centuries of Norse rule, and their ties with Scandinavia have remained strong through fishing and trade. Other parts of Scotland were extensively settled by Norwegians – Caithness and Sutherland, the Western Isles – but the intervening centuries have submerged their Scandinavian character and made them Scottish, their Viking past betrayed only by the many place-names coined by their former overlords. Of all the Viking colonies, Scotland has retained a rich memory of this turbulent and long-lasting episode of her past, embodied in language, history and most of all in the physical remains of houses, graves, weapons, silverwork and more.

This book is concerned with the archaeology of Scandinavian Scotland, how the colonists lived and died, fought and traded. There have been many exciting discoveries over the last hundred years and Scotland's museums contain many fine artefacts, from everyday domestic equipment to silver brooches and the swords and shields of Viking warriors. In the countryside there are the foundations of houses, burial mounds, ruined churches and castles, many in

the care of the State and presented to the visitor as a tangible part of our Norse inheritance. Less than twenty Norse settlements have been identified and excavated, but this is a rich haul compared to other areas of the Norse colonies – if we had a contemporary house for even a fraction of the surviving Scandinavian settlement names, the archaeology of Viking Scotland would be rich indeed.

Some explanation is needed of these terms, Viking, Scandinavian and Norse, for though they may appear to be interchangeable, in fact their meanings are different. Viking, in particular, is such an evocative word that it is often used (as in the title of this book) in a general sense to cover the whole episode of raiding and colonization from Scandinavia. In its strict sense, a viking was a Scandinavian warrior who went out on sea-borne raids. The term Viking Age as used by archaeologists means the period, from about AD 780 to about 1100, during which both raiding and colonization took place and during which there was a distinctive material culture – the same types of artefact were used throughout the Viking world. In Scotland as elsewhere in the Atlantic colonies that culture was Norse, because the settlers were Norwegian. A domesticated viking was a Norseman. Once the Viking Age was over, the next two centuries from AD 1100 to 1300 (or even to 1500 in the Northern Isles) are known to archaeologists as the late Norse period, when Norse influence was still dominant, but the character of material culture

had changed. The term Scandinavian is more general than Norse and refers to Denmark and Sweden as well as Norway. The textbook for the period is Barbara Crawford's *Scandinavian Scotland* (1987), in which Scandinavian is used as an umbrella term for the study of the centuries during which the north and west coasts of Scotland were part of the Scandinavian world. There have been many books written on the Vikings, but very few dealing in any detail with Scotland, perhaps because although the archaeology of Viking Scotland is rich it is as yet relatively little studied.

The start of the adventure

The weather had been improving slowly for a century or two. This was a subtle encourage-

1 *The long sea voes of Shetland were gentler versions of the Norwegian fjords; East Voe of Scalloway, with the sixteenth-century castle of Scalloway in the foreground.*

ment to inventive Norwegian boat-builders, and by the late eighth century they had developed a boat capable of ocean exploration. Calmer seas and sailing boats to skim the waves created the right conditions for the Viking Age, for sea-borne exploits of adventure and discovery, raiding, trading and colonization far beyond the old familiar horizons. Scotland came early into the story, for the Shetland Islands lie only about 180 nautical miles from the west coast of Norway, a mere two days sailing in the spring when the prevailing winds favoured voyages to the west. From Shetland to the green isles of Orkney, and thence south to mainland Caithness or south-west to the Hebrides and ultimately to the Irish Sea, the possibilities were endless. There was good land to be taken in the Scottish islands, in landscapes not so very different from the homeland and not so far away that one need feel homesick, and there would be much coming and going between the two in the years to come.

The essential elements of the Viking sea-going vessel were in place by the late eighth century: strength, lightness, speed, a keel, a sail and ease of beaching. Scandinavia had plenty of good timber for boat-building. Clinker-built boats had been developed in the last centuries BC, providing both strength and elegance of design by means of overlapping planks or strakes, fastened together by iron rivets. A T-shaped keel was introduced and the prow and stern posts were arched higher by about AD 500. The sail was adopted in addition to oars in the seventh century (a late development compared to areas farther south). The steering oar could be swivelled upwards during landing. A shallow draught and strong keel were essential to landing by running the boat up to a flat beach, but in time the demands of trade required deeper vessels which could carry more goods; in response, new trading places developed where deeper water and the construction of quays allowed such ships to tie up and off-load in sufficient depth of water.

The adventurous viking had the means to set off across the sea, but the reasons for the Viking Age are more complex. The urge to explore is ever-present in any human population, and the lure of gold and silver and slaves was irresistible at that time. In addition, younger sons of land-owning Norwegians needed to carve out their own futures; good farming land along the fjords of western Norway was limited. The role of trade should not be underestimated, for Norway had much to offer and the affluent Viking Age encouraged a taste for southern wines and eastern silks and spices. Norwegian exports were mainly perishable: slaves, furs, fish, timber, walrus ivory, reindeer antler and hide ropes, but

soapstone was a major non-perishable commodity. Another important factor in the emergence of the Viking Age was the political situation in Norway. Struggles to establish a unified kingship led to intense rivalries between leading families, causing some to seek safer places to live and others to seek the wealth from plundering overseas that would make them powerful at home.

Scotland was on the fringe of Europe as seen from Charlemagne's France, but the Viking Age made it part of a great North Atlantic community of islands, from Ireland and the Isle of Man northwards to the Faeroes and Iceland and westwards to Greenland and Newfoundland, all of which were linked to some degree with Norway (2). It is likely that the Scottish islands were the first to be colonized, probably soon after 800 — the precise date is uncertain — followed in the mid-ninth century by the Faeroes, the Isle of Man, north-west England and Ireland. Norse settlement in Ireland appears to have been confined to urban trading-stations, suggesting that the native Irish were strong enough to resist rural colonization. After a period of exploratory voyages around 860, Iceland was settled during the decades from 870 to 930, and Greenland was colonized from Iceland around the turn of the century. America was certainly visited by the Norsemen, but it is doubtful whether there was any long-term settlement of the Vinland (Newfoundland) discovered by Leif Eiriksson.

This was a maritime world dependent on boats, whether warships or cargo-boats, but navigation was a risky exercise: there were no sea-charts, no compasses and no knowledge of latitude and longitude. The four cardinal points were understood, along with some astronomy, but the vital ingredient for successful voyages was human experience at sea. Distances were estimated on the basis of shifts at the oars or days of sailing. Landmarks such as mountains that could be seen a long way out to sea were invaluable, as were sea-birds whose presence told of land in the vicinity. Some navigational

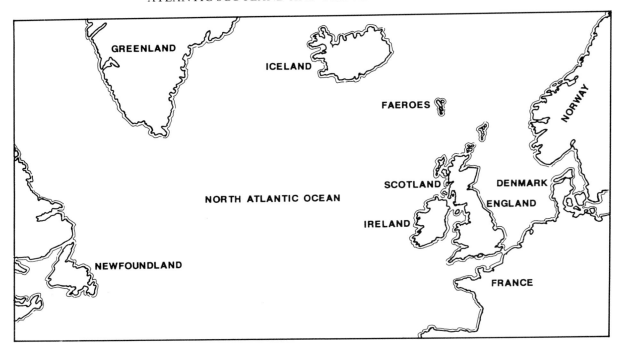

information is preserved in the Icelandic sagas: for instance, sailing directions from Norway to Greenland tell the reader to sail westwards, sufficiently far to the north of the Shetland islands that they were sighted only in good weather and sufficiently far to the south of the Faeroes that the mountains remained half-way below the horizon, and to steer so far south of Iceland that no land could be seen, but coastal sea-birds and mammals could be observed. One story makes very clear the uncertain nature of Viking navigation: King Olaf of Norway instructed an Icelandic captain to take an exile to Greenland, but the captain protested that he had never been to Greenland. The king replied that it would be good experience, but, in case the ship failed to make it to Greenland, the exile was to be left in Iceland or Scotland – and if that proved too difficult, he was to be thrown overboard, for on no account was he to be brought back to Norway. Stories such as these belong to the heyday of Norse exploration, when a common pool of knowledge and experience had developed; in the early days of the Viking expansion westwards, there must have been even more trial and error.

The word Viking is such a powerful and emotive term today, reflecting both the fear that they generated at the time and the romantic image portrayed in more recent periods through literature and film, that it can come as a surprise that the inhabitants of Britain who were harassed in the late eighth and ninth centuries called them not Vikings but gentiles (pagans) or *gall* (foreigners). Both are terms coined to express the contrast between the alien and the familiar, the enemy and oneself. Over the years there has been much scholarly discussion of the origin and meaning of the word viking. The most commonly accepted explanation is that it derives from the Old Norse *vik*, meaning bay, and that it was coined by the Norwegians themselves to describe a sea-borne pirate who lurked in bays ready to pounce upon passing cargo-ships. In time it came to mean simply a pirate adventurer. The word was certainly used in this way by the compilers of the Icelandic sagas in the thirteenth and fourteenth centuries.

Like all emotive subjects, the Vikings swing between a good press and a bad press; even among academics, there has been a marked cycle in the last few decades in the thinking about Viking Scotland, from a view of unremitting bloodshed and extermination at the hands of the Vikings to a degree of co-existence between native Pict and Scot and the incoming Norsemen. The latter theory, based on archaeological rather than historical evidence, provoked much opposition in the 1970s, but the weight of the evidence is now such that it cannot be discounted (see Chapter 2). Nevertheless, there is the danger of swinging too far and forgetting that the early Viking raiders were committed to outright gain and not to counting human loss – there can have been nothing romantic about suffering a Viking attack on farm or monastery (5). The real point is that there were several stages to the Norse conquest of the Scottish Isles: raiding, colonization and trading, and the latter two stages involved a more subtle relationship than simple 'kill and take', as will be discussed in later chapters.

The nature of the evidence

Scotland is fortunate in the amount of evidence that survives of the Viking Age; there are enough excavated settlements to furnish some real evidence of what happened when the Norsemen began to colonize the islands around 800 and to show how these settlements developed over the next three centuries of the Viking Age proper, and beyond into the local late Norse period, 1100 to 1300. Place-names support and fill out the archaeological picture, indicating with satisfactory reliability the extent and density of

2 *Map of Scotland and the North Atlantic.*

3 *The bleakly beautiful landscape of Iceland; settlers from the Hebrides were involved in the Viking colonization of Iceland.*

Scandinavian settlement; a home-based if not home-grown saga supplements the meagre historical information offered by monastic records. *Orkneyinga Saga*, known originally as *Jarls' Saga* because it is the saga of the *earls* of Orkney, is thought to have been compiled by an Icelander based in Thurso, whose geographic knowledge of the earldom was excellent for the Thurso area and mainland Orkney, but hazy for areas farther afield such as Shetland.

The Norse earldom of Orkney was established towards the end of the ninth century. The 'official' story derived from Icelandic sagas attributes its foundation to the Norwegian king, Harald Finehair. Infuriated by raids on the Norwegian coast by vikings from the Northern and Western Isles of Scotland, Harald led a punitive expedition, ravaging as far south as the Isle of Man. He granted the earldom of Orkney and Shetland to the Norwegian Earl Rognvald of Møre, who in turn, and with the king's approval, gave it to his brother Sigurd. The problem with this neat account is that King Harald had more than enough to manage in trying to keep control of the west coast of Norway, and it seems unlikely that he could afford to go off overseas on such an expedition. Moreover there is no mention of this great voyage of revenge in the contemporary Irish written sources, and the Icelandic sagas were compiled three or four centuries after the event. Other sources, similarly late in date but derived from Norse tradition in Scotland, suggest that the Earl of Møre took the Northern Isles himself and established the earldom of Orkney. This made the Møre family uncomfortably powerful for the Norwegian crown and accounts for the bad relations between the two which are apparent from historical accounts. By the late tenth century the earldom of Orkney included not only Shetland but the northern mainland of Scotland and the Western Isles. There seems also to have

been a degree of Orkney authority in the Isle of Man at this period.

The modern reader who would follow the adventures of the leading Orkneymen of the Viking Age is even more fortunate than any counterpart in the Middle Ages because, as well as the Icelandic sagas, there are the works of twentieth-century authors steeped not only in the sagas but also in the evidence revealed by archaeologists. George Mackay Brown understands how Orkney has become what it is today, a fine mixture of peoples, cultures and histories, and his novels, *Magnus* (1973) and *Vinland* (1992), build on the saga accounts in a most satisfying and acceptable way. Dorothy Dunnett's absorbing novel, *King Hereafter* (1982), expands the bald saga account of the life of Earl Thorfinn. Who can say whether she is right or wrong in identifying Thorfinn with Macbeth, rather than the shadowy Karl Hundason as others would have it? Equally, was Thorfinn's court poet (skald) an Icelander, Arnor Thordarson, or Einhof, the son of Ranald and Ragna of Breckness in Orkney, under an assumed name, as George Mackay Brown would have it in *Vinland*? Do such details matter outside genealogy? A rounded understanding of Viking life is what we need, an impression not just of the lives of great men but of ordinary farmers and their families.

This is where the work of the archaeologist comes to the fore: rubbish heaps and ruined houses tell more of domestic life than the most realistic of contemporary sagas, and graves tell of how people dressed and how their boats were built. This book explores the physical remains of Norse life and death in Scotland, but sometimes the prosaic may mingle with story and history, as when a farm mentioned in the sagas is identified on the ground today. All the evidence relates to people of Norwegian origin, although it is quite possible that Danish Vikings raided the east coast of Scotland and even used Scottish waters to reach the Irish Sea. The attention of Swedish Vikings was concentrated eastwards into Russia and the far east.

4 *Map of the British Isles showing the areas settled by Scandinavians.*

Viking Age archaeology in Scotland should not be confined to the study of the Scandinavian newcomers, for their activities involved the native population and can only be understood in the context of the society that they encountered – the chapter that follows sets the scene for the arrival of the first Vikings in Scotland.

The present location of major finds of Viking artefacts is given in the text, and the abbreviation NMS stands for the National Museums of Scotland in Edinburgh.

5 *An artist's reconstruction of a Viking raid; running their boats on to the beach allowed swift surprise attacks.*

CHAPTER TWO

Scotland before the Vikings

The Viking adventure in Scotland was part of a great Scandinavian enterprise that reached north and west across the Atlantic, south into the Mediterranean and east into Russia – but that is the historian's overview, armed with hindsight. For the individual boatload of Vikings, the pattern was much smaller, local and personal. There was no grand design behind the process of raiding and settlement in Scotland; it must have happened piecemeal, its attractions spread by word of mouth, family by family along the Norwegian seaboard. Only later was a political dimension added, when the earldom of Orkney and Shetland was created a century or so after the adventure began.

We do not know how early settlement as opposed to raiding began, or whether in the Northern Isles the two processes can really be separated, but neither can be understood without consideration of the existing native population of Scotland. It is often suggested that there had been contact between Scotland and Norway long before the Viking Age began, despite a conspicuous lack of either historical or archaeological evidence. Accidental landings by boats blown off course are probably inevitable, but none of the Scandinavian artefacts in Scotland or Celtic artefacts in Norway can be dated earlier than the ninth century, and the same is true of intrusive place-names in both places. Most of the artefacts in Norway identified as imports from the Celtic west, from Scotland or Ireland, are exquisite jewellery or church furnishings such as jewelled mounts torn from gospel-books or richly decorated caskets for the relics of saints. The problem encountered in trying to date such objects is that they became heirlooms, and the date at which they were finally buried may bear little relation to their date of manufacture.

The Vikings were illiterate. Their histories were written in the thirteenth and fourteenth centuries, and there are no contemporary Scandinavian records for their activities in the British Isles in the formative eighth and ninth centuries. The Christian peoples they encountered were, however, literate, at least to the extent that monks were educated and monasteries kept yearly records of significant events. These annals provide us with some vital dates: the monastery on the island of Lindisfarne off the coast of Northumbria was sacked by Vikings in 793, followed by the first of a series of attacks on Iona, the Christian heart of Scotland, in 795. Iona lies off the west coast of the island of Mull in Argyll (6), a perfect base for the Irish missionaries led by Columba in the sixth century and a perfect landfall for Viking raiders on their way to Ireland some two centuries later (7).

The sacking of Iona in 795 is the first recorded raid in Scotland, but it is unlikely to have been the first raid to take place. Many a prosperous farm may have been burned to the ground by then. An entry in the *Annals of Ulster* for 794 bleakly evokes the 'devastation of all the islands of Britain by the gentiles'. The Irish annalists were concerned primarily with events involving

the Church or the lay aristocracy, and the entries are very brief. Even attacks on minor monasteries may not have warranted a mention; certainly no specific site is mentioned by name north of Iona, and yet the Outer Hebrides and the Northern Isles must have suffered long before the Viking longboats penetrated to the Irish Sea. In 795, along with Iona, were devastated, we are informed by the annalist, the island of Skye and monasteries in Ireland; it would be very interesting to know which sites in Skye were involved. Too few native settlements or monastic sites have been excavated anywhere in Scotland to draw any conclusions from the lack of evidence for attack (such as burnt material or human skeletons).

6 *Aerial view of the abbey on Iona; the earthwork enclosure of the early monastery is visible in the foreground.*

Hoards

One spectacular archaeological discovery has been attributed to the Viking threat – the hoard of native silver found in 1958 on St Ninian's Isle in Shetland. Professor Andrew O'Dell from the University of Aberdeen was excavating the ruins of a medieval chapel, which had been built on the site of an earlier chapel, when a local boy, his first day on the dig, lifted a paving stone and revealed a clutch of silver (8). There were 28 objects in all, finely decorated bowls, brooches, sword fittings and other items of silver, buried

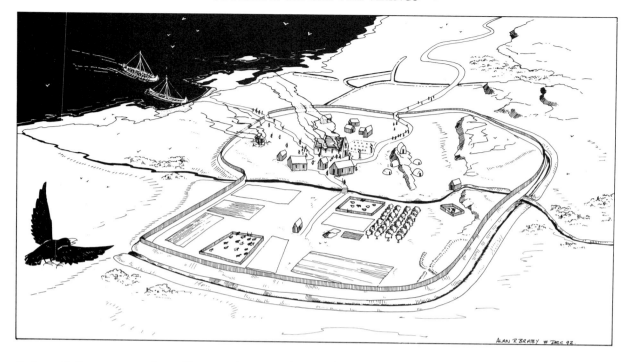

ALAN R BRABY # DEC 92.

7 *An artist's reconstruction of Iona at the time of the first Viking attack in* AD *795.*

8 *Part of the Pictish silver hoard from St Ninian's Isle, Shetland, which included tableware as well as personal jewellery and sword fittings.*

along with part of the jaw of a porpoise in a box of larchwood (most of the box had rotted away).

In the days before safes and banks, the most effective way of hiding valuables was to bury them, and those that remained buried imply that their owners were killed before they could recover them. The monk Blathmac was killed during a Viking attack on Iona in 825 because he refused to reveal where St Columba's relics were buried; his murderers dug here and there in a vain attempt to find the valuable casket containing the relics, but it was retrieved by the monks after they had gone.

The silver treasure of St Ninian's Isle is thought to have been buried for safekeeping beneath the floor of the early chapel sometime around 800, to judge by the date of the objects themselves. The most likely reason for their concealment is a Viking raid. The designs and techniques used to create these silver objects suggest an origin in a Pictish workshop, and the owner is likely to have been either a leading Pictish family living in the vicinity or perhaps the Church itself, if they were gifts.

An even more tantalizing glimpse of the

wealth of secular Pictish society before the Viking onslaught is the hoard of silver and amber discovered at Burgar in Orkney; tantalizing because the treasure can no longer be traced. Found in the early nineteenth century in the ruins of a broch (an Iron Age fortification), the hoard consisted of silver vessels, combs, brooches, dress-pins and chains, together with a number of amber beads of various sizes, but sadly everything has since been lost.

The inhabitants of Scotland

Who were the Picts and other peoples whom the Vikings encountered in Scotland? Unlike the Faeroes and Iceland, Scotland presented a fully, if in places sparsely, occupied landscape, farmed by people whose overall level of culture mirrored that of early medieval Europe. Most of Scotland north of the Clyde–Forth estuaries belonged to the Picts, apart from the western area of Argyll and the inner Hebrides as far north perhaps as Skye, which formed the Scottish kingdom of Dalriada. The Scots were originally Irish families from the tribe of the Scotti in Co. Antrim, who had been colonizing western Scotland since the early centuries AD. By the eighth century there existed a long history of warfare, co-operation and intermarriage between Dalriada and Pictland. The Picts had the greater right to the land that was to become Scotland, because they were the descendants of the indigenous Celtic tribes who had successfully thwarted the Roman army, whereas the Scots were newcomers.

The British kingdom of Strathclyde was still a force in its own right in the late eighth century, with a power-centre on the fortified Dumbarton Rock, looming over the waterway of the Clyde. South of the Firth of Forth lived a mixed population of indigenous Britons and intrusive Anglians, the latter representing the northern limit of political control by the kingdom of Northumbria. To the west, Anglian dominance stretched along the coastal plain at least beyond Whithorn, where a Northumbrian bishopric had been established in the early eighth century. The Rhins of Galloway had long been settled by Irish incomers, identified almost solely by their numerous Gaelic place-names. The population of south-west Scotland was thus a mixture of Britons, Irish and Anglians, originally speaking Brittonic, Gaelic and Old English respectively but by the late eighth century probably thoroughly mixed both in blood and tongue and with the common bond of Christianity between them.

The first people whom the Vikings encountered in the Northern Isles were Picts, while in the Hebrides they were likely to find both Picts and Scots. Archaeology cannot produce as precise dates as those in the annals, but an estimate at least can be made of excavated sites likely to have been in use at the time of the first Viking raids. In the Hebrides a small village existed at the Udal on the sandy grasslands at the north end of the island of North Uist, and this was subsequently replaced by a Norse settlement. The native houses were built in a distinctive figure-of-eight plan which has also been found in Co. Antrim and in Orkney and which seems to be one of several cultural links between Ireland, the Hebrides and the Northern Isles in pre-Norse times. The seaways up and down the west coast of Scotland and into the Irish Sea were well travelled before the Vikings made them their own; some passages were notoriously dangerous, and perhaps Norwegian skippers commandeered native expertise. Slaves in any form were fair merchandise, and a navigator, who could also act as interpreter, would have been very useful. The story about the monk Blathmac on Iona points to the essential need either to learn some Gaelic or to acquire an interpreter. Blathmac had to be interrogated on the subject of the whereabouts of the monastery's valuables, whether or not the Vikings understood the significance or indeed the existence of St Columba's reliquary.

The social pattern seems to have been one of individual farms, such as A Cheardach Mhor on South Uist, and small communities of several houses, as at the Udal. As in most periods of

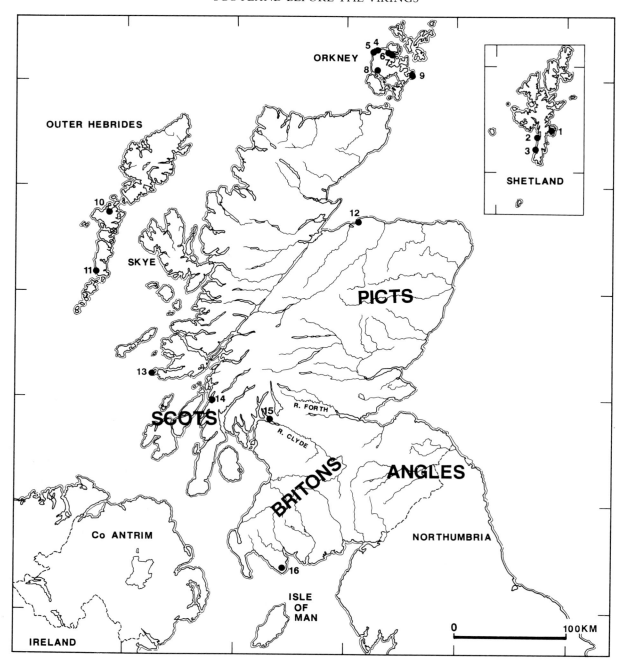

prehistory in Scotland, more evidence of pre-Norse domestic settlement has been discovered in Orkney than elsewhere, particularly as a result of excavations over the last twenty years or so. In many cases sites were revealed by coastal erosion, and the original extent of the settlement is

9 Map of Scotland around AD 800 with places mentioned in the text. 1 Culbinsgarth; 2 Papil; 3 St Ninian's Isle; 4 Buckquoy; 5 Brough of Birsay; 6 Burgar; 7 Gurness; 8 Howe; 9 Skaill; 10 The Udal; 11 A Cheardach Mhor; 12 Burghead; 13 Iona; 14 Dunadd; 15 Dumbarton Rock; 16 Whithorn.

often difficult to judge. The Pictish farm at Buckquoy in Orkney appeared to have been an isolated farm when it was excavated in 1970–1, but subsequent excavation in 1978 uncovered another contemporary house some 100m (330ft) away at Red Craig, and there may well have been others in the vicinity. Single farmsteads have been excavated at Skaill in Deerness and at Gurness, and on a crannog-like structure at Bretta Ness on Rousay, whereas the Pictish phases at Howe near Stromness and at Pool on Sanday represented larger social units, though neither warrants the term village. There was a large, open, paved area at Pool, which may have been a meeting-place (**10**).

Most of the excavated houses of this period are no longer visible, but an excellent example of a Pictish house may be seen at Gurness in Orkney

(**11, 12A**). Scattered over the moorlands of Caithness and Sutherland there are ruined buildings known locally as wags; these are circular or rectangular houses with internal stone pillars which helped to support their roofs. There has been little excavation but what dating evidence exists suggests that this type of building belongs to the early historic period, in the middle and later first millennium AD.

The Picts and Scots built both round and rectangular houses, sometimes combining round and rectangular rooms in one dwelling. The feasting-halls of their warlords were large rectangular structures built of stone or timber or a mixture of both, and these would have been

10 *Pictish buildings and paved area at Pool, Sanday.*

11 *Aerial view of the broch settlement at Gurness, Orkney; the Pictish house is in the foreground.*

instantly recognizable to a Viking. The society that they encountered would also have been familiar to the Vikings as similar to their own: it was a hierarchical society, ranging from kings and chiefs to farmworkers and slaves. The social strata are to some extent visible on native sites, for as well as farms of various sizes there are forts: small forts for minor chiefs and larger forts for regional rulers and high kings. Largest of all was the great Pictish fort at Burghead on the south coast of the Moray Firth. The distribution of forts known to date from this period is markedly coastal, underlining the importance of the sea for transport and trade. We know from historical sources of battles fought at sea and of seaborne expeditions, and it is clear that both Picts and Scots had much maritime expertise.

24

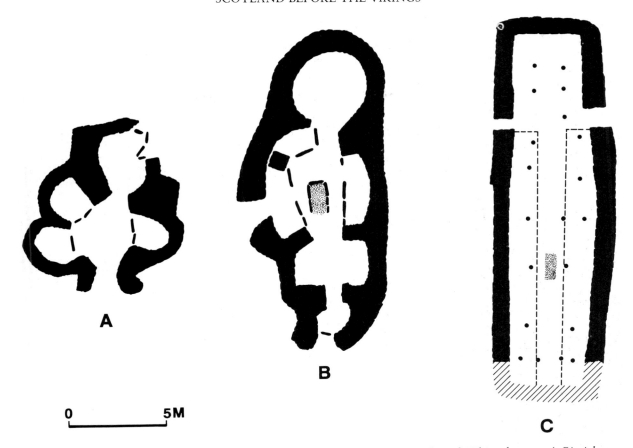

A

B

0   5M

C

12 *Plans of Pictish and Viking houses. A Pictish Gurness; B Pictish Buckquoy; C Viking Jarlshof.*

Archaeological evidence of their boats is unfortunately sparse, but it points to the use of clinker-built boats as well as skin-boats and logboats (the latter probably used mostly on inland waters), and there is evidence to suggest that the Picts at least may have adopted the sail long before it came into use in Scandinavia.

The single most important difference between the Vikings and the peoples whom they encountered in Scotland was religion. The Vikings were pagan, worshipping a pantheon of gods, whereas Scotland was part of the Christian world, open to the many civilizing influences of early medieval Christendom.

The Vikings seem to have recognized the strength of native culture and to have responded with an instinctive need to dominate rather than to obliterate. In virtually every case, Viking settlements were built literally on top of earlier native farms. Rebuilding on the same spot was a familiar device in Norway to avoid taking more land out of farming use, but there was no shortage of good land among the Scottish islands and another explanation is needed. In effect, the Vikings were taking over existing patterns of land ownership and administration, and this is particularly clear at Birsay in Orkney, a Pictish power-base which fell early into Viking hands. Not only were farms round the Bay of Birsay and the high-status island settlement on the Brough of Birsay (13) taken over, but individual house-plots on the Brough were retained.

What is not clear is precisely how this happened. The nature of the relationship between native and Norseman at the time of the Viking colonization has been the subject of much heated discussion over the last twenty years,

13 *The Point of Buckquoy and the Brough of Birsay; the low mound beneath the track in the left foreground covered the Pictish and Viking site of Buckquoy.*

since the traditional view of violent extermination or at best slavery at the hands of the Vikings was challenged by new archaeological evidence. In the summers of 1970 and 1971, a low mound at the edge of the cliff on the Point of Buckquoy at Birsay was excavated, revealing the basal courses of stone walls, paved floors and hearths. The mound had been formed by the ruins of a Norse farm which had itself been built on top of the ruins of an earlier Pictish farm, and into the top of the mound had been dug the grave of a tenth-century Norseman, conveniently providing dating evidence for the domestic layers below. Much of the site had already fallen into the sea, with the result that only a partial picture of the Pictish and Norse farms survived. Three phases of the Norse farm could be seen, each represented by a different kind of building: the final phase was represented by part of a dwelling-house, the second phase by a small threshing-barn and the earliest by a byre. In each phase there must have been other buildings which have long since vanished into the sea, and there may

have been other intermediate phases not represented at all in what survived. What did survive implied a minimum of three building phases which have to be fitted in between the earliest likely date for Norse settlement around 800 and the last possible date at which the final dwelling-house might have been demolished in order to allow time for the ruins to become the mound in which was buried the Viking grave. This was dated to the third quarter of the tenth century by an unworn but halved Anglo-Saxon coin of 940–6.

The Viking farm must have been established early in the ninth century, perhaps very early. The Pictish farm had flourished in the seventh and early eighth century, and appeared to have been abandoned for some time before the

Vikings began to build, or at least that part of it which survived appeared to have been abandoned. Thus far the story seemed reasonable enough. The problem came when it was realized that the artefacts from the Norse domestic levels were not Scandinavian types but normal native Pictish types of tiny bone pins and decorated bone combs (14, 15). They implied that the Viking newcomers were able to obtain domestic equipment from a native population which had not been exterminated. This, together with evidence elsewhere for Norsemen adopting native customs, including Christianity in the ninth century, suggested that the traditional idea of what happened had been too black-and-white in its approach, and that some degree of integration of the two communities must have taken place in Orkney if not elsewhere.

Opponents of this idea have cited the traditional historical view of the Vikings as bloodthirsty thugs, despite allowing for just that social integration to have taken place on the Isle of Man (where the lack of female pagan graves has been accepted as evidence that the Vikings intermarried with the local girls, see Chapter 5). The evidence from the Udal on North Uist has also been used in an attempt to demolish the idea of social integration: here the eighth-century native settlement was apparently replaced by one characterized by an entirely Scandinavian culture. This is just one site, however, and as yet unpublished in detail. In contrast, in Orkney, all the excavations that have taken place since Buckquoy have told the same story: so much blending of Norse and native culture that it is impossible to envisage a situation in which the Norsemen either killed or enslaved the entire population.

According to saga evidence, the Norse in Scotland, or at least those in the heart of the earldom in Orkney, were forced to adopt Christianity in 995 by the Norwegian King Olaf Tryggvason. Arriving in Orkney after an eventful four years of looting around the British Isles, during which he was himself baptised in the Scilly Isles and married in England to an Irish

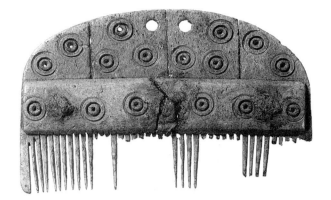

14 *Pictish comb from Viking Buckquoy.*

15 *Pictish pin from Viking Buckquoy.*

princess, Olaf requested a word with Earl Sigurd Hlodvisson. 'I want you and all your subjects to be baptised. If you refuse, I'll have you killed on the spot, and I swear that I'll ravage every island with fire and steel' (*Orkneyinga Saga*, chapter 12). With the understatement that makes the Saga such a joy to read, we are told that 'the earl could see what kind of situation he was in' and that he promptly accepted baptism.

There is in fact evidence to suggest that the Norsemen had already begun to embrace Christianity before the ardent convert, Olaf, arrived, even if the earls themselves had not. Early Scandinavian place-names incorporating the element kirk from Old Norse *kirkja*, church, are to be found in the Northern Isles, as in Kirkbister and Kirkabister. It is likely that not every Norse immigrant had a Norwegian wife to bring to the new colony and that local Pictish girls became wives to the incomers, or nurses to their children, and that Christianity would soon become absorbed by the Norse population. Significantly, analysis of the surviving folktales of the Northern Isles has shown that their origins lie in pre-Norse tales rather than in Scandinavian stories; this must surely indicate the strength of influence of the hand that rocked the cradle.

The Picts had a tradition of fine stone-carving which reached its heights of technique and elaborate design in a Christian context in the eighth and early ninth centuries (**16**). A curious contrast between Orkney and Shetland is that there appears to have been a break in the sequence of Orcadian sculpture around 800, the time of the earliest Viking settlement, whereas in Shetland sculpture continued through the ninth and into the tenth and eleventh centuries, making a smooth transition from Pictish to Picto-Viking and thence to Norse sculpture. This must reflect a difference in the intensity of early Norse settlement, the larger number of colonists being attracted by Orkney, both for its fertile land and for its proximity to the rest of the British Isles. Two Shetland cross-slabs are particularly interesting. One was found in the churchyard at Culbinsgarth on the island of Bressay off the east coast of mainland Shetland (**17**), and it bears an inscription in ogam (a type of writing invented in Ireland and used in Pictland and elsewhere in Britain); the inscription includes not only the Gaelic words for cross and son but also the Norse word for daughter. This is a neat demonstration of the cultural mix that existed then in Shetland, and it also implies that some Norsemen had adopted Christianity.

16 *Pictish cross-slab in Aberlemno churchyard, Angus.*

An earlier stone, dating probably from around 800, was found in the churchyard at Papil on the island of West Burra off the west coast of mainland Shetland (**18**). The design of this cross-slab is so similar to and yet better executed than the stone from Bressay, that the latter is likely to have been modelled on it. On the Papil stone is a pair of bird-headed and bird-legged human figures with a human head between their beaks. The general motif is a common one in Christian iconography, but the two extraordinary bird-men are unique and it is clear that the bird-men were carved by a different hand to the rest of the slab. Why? The place-name Papil comes from the Old Norse word *papa* for priest – but in Iceland the same word *papa* is used as a nickname for the puffin. An Icelandic scholar has suggested that the Papil bird-men were added to the stone by Norsemen, poking fun at church-

17 *Cross-slab from Culbinsgarth, Bressay, Shetland; the design of this multi-lingual stone is based on the earlier stone from Papil (18).*

18 *Cross-slab from Papil, Shetland; beneath the clerics with their book-satchels is the lion symbol of St Mark. The birdmen may be a later addition.*

men and creating an appropriate play on both the name of the place and the Christian motif. If this engaging idea is accepted, it implies quite a high level of literacy or at the very least an unusual sense of humour.

CHAPTER THREE

Viking Age Scotland
AD 780–1100

The story of Viking Scotland is very much the province of the archaeologist. There are some historical sources, which provide a few dates and the names and achievements of famous people. There are also linguistic sources, chiefly place-names, which chart the extent of Scandinavian success in Scotland, but the details of life and death come from the material remains, ideally from excavation but often from chance discoveries. The latter are often what makes the Vikings such an exciting and absorbing subject, with the unexpected discovery of a rich boat-burial or the sudden appearance in a saleroom catalogue of Viking treasure. The total picture of Viking life depends upon slow and meticulous study of all its aspects: building design, burial ritual, the products of industry and trade, or the contents of the rubbish heap.

The sagas

Although the Vikings themselves were illiterate in the early years of their adventure overseas, apart from the basic recording of trade and revenue, the Christian peoples whom they encountered had scribes in their monasteries whose duties included recording the events of the year, at least so far as they concerned the Church or the secular state. The monastic annals provide a bare chronological framework for Scotland, primarily from the *Annals of Ulster*, which has the merit of being contemporary with the events recorded. The major historical source for the

Norse earldom of Orkney, Caithness, Shetland and the Western Isles lies in the Icelandic sagas, primarily *Orkneyinga Saga* but also *Landnáma-bók*, *Egil's Saga*, *Magnus' Saga* and others. But the historical value of these sagas varies and is not always easy to define. At best they convey an impression of political life in the eleventh and twelfth centuries, at worst they may be misleading in failing to distinguish between anachronistic oral tradition and contemporary society.

The account in *Orkneyinga Saga* (chapter 106) of Svein Asleifarson's viking exploits in the mid-twelfth century is a good example:

> In the spring he had more than enough to occupy him, with a great deal of seed to sow which he saw to carefully himself. Then when that job was done, he would go off plundering in the Hebrides and in Ireland on what he called his 'spring-trip', then back home just after midsummer, where he stayed till the cornfields had been reaped and the grain was safely in. After that he would go off raiding again, and never came back till the first month of winter was ended. This he used to call his 'autumn-trip'.

This is a wonderful account of the viking life-style, but is it entirely anachronistic at a period when we know raiding was no longer a normal part of life, or is it a tongue-in-cheek tale about a Viking eccentric who was still living the life of his berserk forebears? Either way, for us and probably for those sitting round the fire more than eight centuries ago, the story remains the best glimpse into the realities of combining the

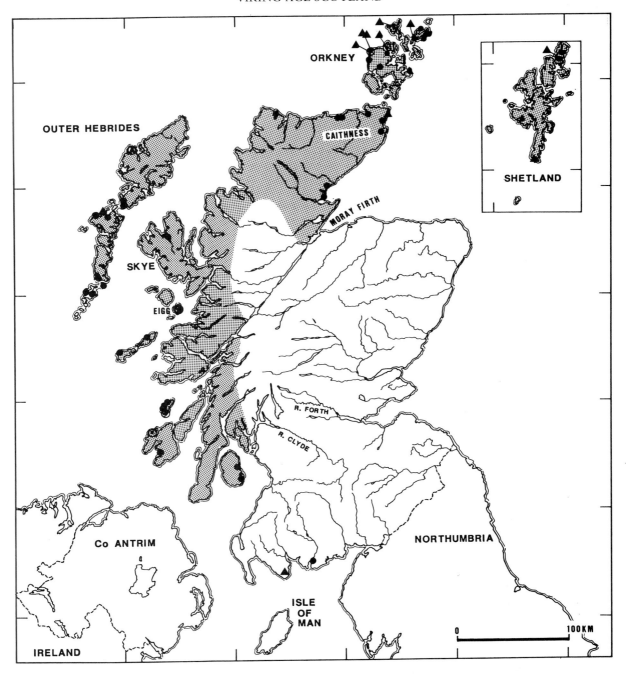

19 *Map of Scotland showing the distribution of Scandinavian place-names (stippled), Viking graves (dots) and cemeteries (ringed dots), and Viking settlements (triangles). (For Scandinavian place-names in southern Scotland see* **82.***)*

31

Viking life with the exigencies of life on the family farm.

Place-name evidence

The most important non-archaeological source of information is the linguistic study of place-names. The Ordnance Survey map of any area of Scotland today carries an immense heritage of linguistic activity, recording in the parish, village, farm, hill, valley and coastal names the history of human activity and, for our purposes, the history of Viking colonization. Place-names relate so instantly to people that they are irresistible. In Scotland they mostly reflect the linguistic compromise that took place when the language of the new overlords was absorbed into the linguistic landscape of the native people, except in the Northern Isles where the overwhelming strength of Norse settlement by the end of the ninth century had the effect of obliterating pre-Viking place-names almost entirely.

At one time it was thought that analysis of place-name elements could be used to date the progress of Norse colonization during the ninth and tenth centuries, but linguists have come to be more pessimistic about the limitations of their material and to recognize that precise dating is impossible. Nevertheless, place-names have enormous value both in recording the extent of Norse settlement and as local information about its character and the people involved. Place-names and archaeology agree in identifying the Northern Isles, Caithness and the Western Isles as the most densely settled areas, with considerable Norse influence on the adjacent areas of the northern and western mainland and in southwest Scotland. The place-names in all these areas will be examined more fully in later chapters.

Archaeological evidence

The problems encountered by linguists in dating place-names run parallel to similar problems facing the archaeologist. It is essential to be aware of the nuances of the evidence, seeking to define the legitimate inferences that can be drawn from the material remains of the past. It is no longer acceptable, if it ever was, to make sweeping statements, based on archaeological evidence, which sound as if they are historical fact – to claim, for instance, that oval brooches, because they were a distinctively Scandinavian product, were not worn by local women in Scotland but only by immigrant Scandinavian wives and daughters. This is to ignore the heirloom factor, made more potent by circumstances in the Atlantic colonies which meant that access to Norwegian markets for replacements was limited. Who can deny the possibility of a scenario in which a Viking and his wife (and his daughter if you wish) settle in the Western Isles, and their son marries a local woman who is pleased to inherit and to be buried wearing her mother-in-law's brooches? Does it matter which way we interpret the evidence of that grave? It does, not in the context of the immediate family which, even with the addition of a local woman, was still an essentially Scandinavian social unit, but because our interpretation subtly changes the balance of our view of Viking Scotland from one in which intermarriage and interaction with the native population is inconceivable to a more realistic view in which both are possible and indeed likely.

Viking Age Scotland resembles the Faeroes and Iceland in its economic development, rather than Ireland and England, despite the close links with Ireland. No trading towns developed in Scandinavian Scotland to mirror Dublin and York. It is often suggested that Pierowall in Westray may have been Orkney's trading station, on account of the cemetery found there, the natural harbour and Westray's position on the route from Norway and Shetland westwards. The cemetery is no longer unique, however, and there is no indication in *Orkneyinga Saga*, where it is mentioned once, that Pierowall was specially important, although its Norse name, *Hofn* or haven, reflects its usefulness as a harbour. The *Saga* mentions Kirkwall as a market town of 'only a few houses' in the mid-eleventh century, implying an essentially local function.

The absence of trading stations may be related in part to the pre-Norse situation. The centres of power in Pictland and Dalriada, which have been identified as possible emporia in the sixth to eighth centuries, lie outside the area of Norse settlement in the ninth and tenth centuries and their trading activities appear to have been curtailed by the Viking presence in their sea-ways. Dunollie and Dunadd were Scottish strongholds which were abandoned when the Scottish royal dynasty moved eastwards into Pictland around 843, and the great Pictish fort at Burghead on the southern shore of the Moray coast is likely to have been in decline even before Viking activities severed its trade with the Northern Isles (though it was still worth attacking in the ninth century).

This is not to deny that there were long-distance contacts between the Norse settlements and the wider medieval world, but rather to emphasize the rural nature of those settlements. The archaeological pattern is one of scattered farms, some clearly more important than others, though the low level of discovery may be over-emphasizing the dominance of individual and widely dispersed farms. The Birsay Bay Project in Orkney has demonstrated that intense archaeological activity in one small area may fill the gaps in the known distribution of settlement by producing evidence of additional sites.

Nevertheless, a pattern of individual farms is precisely the overall impression of settlement given by the Sagas, although it must be remembered that the saga-writers were only concerned with the residences of important families. *Orkneyinga Saga* mentions a hamlet on Westray (chapter 56), no longer extant when the saga was written, but this is an exception. Jarlshof in Shetland is sometimes described by modern writers as a 'township', but this is based on a misunderstanding of the multi-phase plan of the site; the archaeological reality is that this was a successful farm belonging to a moderately extended family. Archaeologists spend much of their time dealing with abandoned settlements which failed for some economic or social reason, but at Jarlshof the Norse farm appears to have been a success that was rebuilt as a medieval farm in the fourteenth century.

Layout of a Viking farm

A typical farm of the ninth and tenth centuries consisted of a small cluster of rectangular buildings: dwelling house, byre and barn were essential elements, often with stone paving between them to reduce the problems of mud in poor weather (20). The dwelling had an earthen floor for warmth, although there might be paving inside the entrance where the wear from the passage of feet was most concentrated; it was designed as one large room or hall, but one end might be screened off as the kitchen. There was a large central hearth, sometimes built with a stone kerb, and low platforms or benches lined the two long walls on either side of the hearth. Traces of these platforms usually survive as lines of stones marking their inner edges, for the surface would have been wooden planking which rots away under normal conditions.

Only the basal courses of the walls survive for the most part; occasionally the long walls appear to have been slightly bowed, but most buildings were straight-sided and the true boat-shaped house is not found in Scotland. The walls were built of stone, earth and turf, usually with a good inner face of stone, a core of earth and rubble and an outer face of turf or stone. Evidence of the use of alternate courses of stone and turf has been found only at Jarlshof, and even there its use was very restricted. Gabled end-walls were sometimes built of solid stone.

Little hint of roofing survives apart from a double row of post-holes running the length of the house and representing internal support; sometimes the posts stood on padstones rather than in holes and these are even more difficult to identify. The posts imply a ridged timber frame, on which a covering of turf or thatch is likely, with thin flagstones protecting the roof-timbers

at the wall-head. The two ends of the roof could be either gabled or hipped, and both are shown in the reconstruction drawings here: gabled ends are vertical, while hipped are angled inwards. Apart from the hearth and the platforms, the internal furnishings of such a dwelling are even more a matter of conjecture, but it seems reasonable to assume that warmth and comfort were important, with furs and woollen rugs on the platforms, brightly coloured wall-hangings and wooden screens at the bench-ends to cut down the draught from the door. Light would come from the fire, the open door and stone lamps in which the wick floated in oil.

The function of subsidiary buildings is not always easy to determine: paving on either side of a central drain and a doorway in the end-wall can reasonably be interpreted as evidence of a byre, but a paved floor alone may indicate either a stable or a threshing-barn. Small square buildings with large central hearths have been interpreted as bath-houses or saunas at Brough of Birsay and Jarlshof, and would certainly be appropriate to the special status of the Birsay settlement (see Chapter 4).

In time this layout of separate dwelling and outhouses changed, first by adding the byre on to the lower end of the dwelling, thus creating the true longhouse in which humans and animals lived under the same roof. This design continued

20 *An artist's reconstruction of a typical early Viking farm.*

the early Norse settlements comes from excavations over the last two decades in Orkney. Modern techniques of large-scale retrieval, particularly wet sieving, are very successful in extracting as much small organic matter as possible from midden deposits, including tiny fishbones, rodent bones and burnt cereal grains. Laboratory analysis of samples from middens reveals microscopic remains such as fragments of insect-wings and plant pollen. Detailed information like this allows a picture to be built up of diet, living conditions and the overall natural environment. Similar information exists for both Caithness and Shetland, as well as Orkney, in the late Norse period (Chapter 7), but elsewhere the published data is scanty.

Organic remains from early Norse settlements in Orkney reveal a mixed agricultural and pastoral economy very similar to that of the native population. Cereal cultivation included both barley and oats; flax was also grown, most probably for its fibres which could be made into linen. Other plants were gathered, such as heather which could be used for bedding, for fuel, for twisting into ropes to hold down the thatched roofs or even as a building material for composite walls in outhouses.

Crowberries were probably eaten, and various herbs would have been used both for flavouring and as medicines. Peat was an invaluable fuel, releasing what little native timber could be found for structural purposes; the supply of larger timber depended upon ample driftwood and imported stocks from mainland Scotland and Norway. Twigs and branches of willow were burnt as fuel on the Birsay sites, implying that there was at least some scrub woodland in the vicinity, unlike the entirely open landscape of today.

Thanks to a slightly warmer climate then than today, reaching a peak around 1000, cereal cultivation on the fertile soils of Orkney was relatively easy, and flour is recorded as an export in Norse times. Breeding livestock was probably more important, certainly during the early pioneering days of the settlement, and most sites

in use into the present century in the Northern and Western Isles and had considerable advantages: not only did the presence of the cows add to the warmth of the house, but the fumes from their urine protected the humans from respiratory diseases. By the twelfth century, additional rooms were added to the long walls of the dwelling.

Economy

Most of the available information about the economic life and environmental conditions of yield bones of cattle, sheep and pigs. The proportions of animals found at Buckquoy are typical: 50 per cent cattle, 30 per cent sheep and 12 per cent pig (the remaining 8 per cent consisted of other mammals). All these animals were useful in several ways, providing meat, leather and hides, and bone as a material for making tools, dress-pins and hair-pins; in addition, cattle and sheep could be used for dairy products and sheep may have yielded wool for textiles, although they were a small and primitive type of sheep whose 'wool' was probably more hair than true wool.

Sheep could be overwintered out of doors, and it may be that the milder climate allowed a longer season in the field for cattle, but the presence of byres at Buckquoy and Jarlshof implies that shelter was needed both for dairying and against the full rigours of winter. This in turn means that the hay harvest was essential for winter feed. Most cattle were slaughtered before maturity, perhaps to meet demand for meat and hides but perhaps also to reduce the number of animals requiring shelter over the winter. The same pattern of slaughter while young applies to the sheep and pigs, and is probably again related to the supply of food and raw materials. A small number of goats appear to have been kept, but it is notoriously difficult to distinguish the bones of goats from those of sheep, particularly primitive types of sheep.

For the most part, the Norse settlers appear to have acquired their livestock locally, but the modern sheep of North Ronaldsay, famous for living on a diet of seaweed, are thought to be descended from Scandinavian stock. Some small mammals may have been imported unwittingly: genetic work on the modern small mammal population of the Outer Hebrides suggests that field mice and cats are derived from Scandinavian stock which, like their human counterparts, overwhelmed the locals. Bones of horses have been found on Viking sites and could have been obtained locally; the horse played an important part in the Pictish life-style and was a frequent motif on symbol stones and other sculpture.

Small numbers of red and roe deer bones have been found, but the hunting of wild mammals appears to have been of minor importance, although *Orkneyinga Saga* mentions hunting grouse and hares as well as deer. Deer antler was certainly appreciated as a tough material for tool-handles and combs, but it can be obtained from seasonally shed antlers and need not involve hunting. The carcasses of seals and whales, washed up on the beaches, must have been greeted with excitement; fresh they provided a change of diet and a source of oil, and even long dead they were an excellent source of bone, particularly the whale, whose massive bones could be used as building materials as well as for smaller items. Part of a whale's rib was used as a cutting block on the Brough of Birsay. Seals may have been hunted, but whale hunting is unlikely.

Seabirds were certainly hunted, for the bones of immature auks and cormorants, which must have been taken from the nest, have been found; eggshells have yet to be identified in archaeological contexts but eggs are likely to have been collected from the nest as well. Seabirds most commonly represented in bone samples include gannets, fulmars, Manx shearwaters, shags, cormorants and great northern divers. Domestic fowl and geese were kept as a source of meat, eggs and feathers, just as they had been kept in the pre-Norse period.

Most Norse settlements in Scotland as elsewhere in the Atlantic colonies were situated beside or within easy access to the sea, and the sea was itself an invaluable source of food. Analysis of fishbones shows that people fished both from the shore and from boats well out to sea, but the bulk of fish was caught offshore: saithe, cod, ling, hake and ballan wrasse. In the early phases of Norse settlement, fishing appears to have been on a small-scale family basis, but there is growing evidence for regular deep-sea fishing in later times (Chapter 7). Allied to fishing was shellfish collection, because limpets were probably used as fishbait rather than food, except in times of food shortage. Limpets and the more easily digestible winkle are the most commonly encountered shellfish on archaeological sites, but their interpretation as a food source is complicated by later recorded traditions: in recent centuries in Scotland limpets and winkles were eaten only as a last resort in times of famine, while in the Faeroes people refused on principle to eat any shellfish. At any period prior to relatively recent times, shellfish are more likely to have been a food of the poor than of the wealthy.

The picture that emerges from all this analysis of organic remains is one of independent, self-sufficient family farms, balancing their individual economic life-styles between agriculture, stock-breeding and fishing, along with hunting and gathering in the time-honoured way. Trading would mostly be done at second hand through merchants, exchanging one commodity for another or for silver bullion, but in the early days of the colonization most imported items would have arrived in the personal baggage of the settlers. They would soon have discovered that their beloved soapstone (steatite) was available in Shetland and need not be imported from the homeland. The soapstone industry flourished in Shetland during the Viking Age and beyond. Large-scale timber would have had to be imported into the islands of Scotland, probably from Norway into the Northern Isles (the archaeological evidence from Tuquoy is discussed further below) and from mainland Scotland into the Western Isles. The earls often obtained their warships from Norway, but there must have been an industry in boat-building in the Scottish colony as well. When in 1878 a peat bog was drained on the western island of Eigg, two shaped stem-posts were found and are believed to date from Viking times; each is made from a single block of oak and was designed to form the stern of the boat, the inner edges stepped to fit the strakes or side-planks.

Much of the domestic equipment needed is likely to have been produced on site; bone-working skills, for instance, would be taught to sons and spinning and weaving to daughters.

Metalworking is likely to have been a specialized craft even in rural areas; an iron smithy has been excavated on the Brough of Birsay in Orkney, and a smith was buried along with his tools at Ballinaby on Islay.

At Tuquoy, Westray, part of a very large pit was excavated recently, which contained a deposit 0.6m (2ft) thick of waterlogged Viking material – an exciting moment for the archaeologists because waterlogged conditions preserve organic remains which normally rot away. It consisted of straw, animal dung and ash and appears to have been the midden and animal bedding of a tenth-century farm. Amongst the rubbish were woodworking debris, wooden artefacts and willow twigs and branches; offcuts of pine suggest large-scale import of trimmed pine trunks from Norway, while larch and spruce offcuts indicate use of driftwood, and fragments of oak and ash point to specialist demand for woods particularly suited to certain types of article. A handle made of maple was probably a personal belonging brought to Orkney from Norway and is an interesting addition to the many bone and metal imports from graves and settlements in Scotland which are typically Scandinavian in origin. A verse in *Orkneyinga Saga* (chapter 94) includes the line 'Excellent the aim of the elm-bows'.

Middens are home to all sorts of insects and the Tuquoy pit had preserved a highly informative collection: outdoor insects from wetland habitats, insects that love warm, rotting matter, animal parasites and human lice and fleas. This sort of insect population is typical of well-preserved organic deposits found elsewhere (in urban Viking York and Dublin, for example) and was probably an inevitable aspect of life for most people, especially in houses that sheltered both people and animals. The contemporary farm at Tuquoy has yet to be found.

Graves

A wide variety of Viking pagan graves appears in the Scottish archaeological record, from the

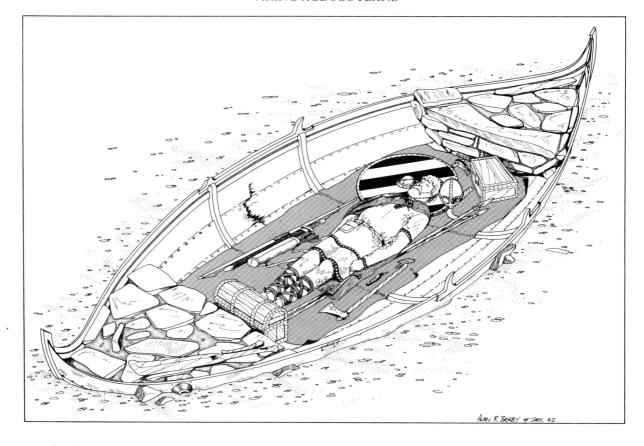

ALAN R BRABY # DEC 92

simple dug grave to the formal boat-burial, and their grave-goods show a similar range from the humble to the splendid. One of the most interesting aspects to emerge in recent years has a bearing on the question of the relationship between the Vikings and the indigenous population: both at Westness and on the Point of Buckquoy in Orkney, the Norse graves were added to existing Pictish cemeteries. With hindsight the same was probably true of the cemetery at Pierowall in Westray, where one recorded grave contained a crouched burial with no grave-goods and where there were other unrecorded graves. In the same way as taking over existing settlement sites, using native burial-places may have served both to underline the supremacy of the incomers and to utilize the existing social organization. Familiarity with Pictish burial customs may also explain the occasional adoption by Vikings of the square or rectangular

21 An artist's reconstruction of a Viking boat-burial; most, but not all, boat-burials were for men.

stone setting round the grave, as at Kiloran Bay in Colonsay and at Pierowall.

Cemeteries of three or more pagan graves have been identified in Orkney at Pierowall, Westness and the Point of Buckquoy, in Caithness at Reay, and in the Hebrides at Valtos in Lewis and Ballinaby in Islay. In the case of Valtos and the Point of Buckquoy the graves were found piecemeal in recent years, suggesting that other cases of apparently isolated graves may also be parts of cemeteries.

Burials within or beneath boats were a Viking speciality, although not as common as popularly assumed nor, in Scotland, as spectacular as those found in Norway at Oseberg and Gokstad. Only four sites in Scotland have produced acceptable

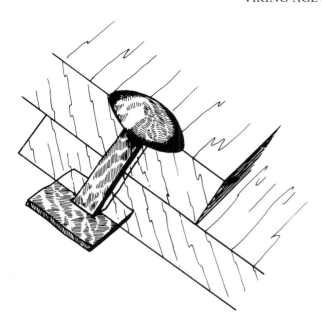

22 *A boat rivet showing how the planks of a boat were fastened together.*

Although both inhumation and cremation were practised in Scandinavia, the normal burial rite in Scotland is inhumation, perhaps because of the shortage of timber on most of the islands where graves have been found. There is no problem in distinguishing a Viking pagan grave from the graves of the native population because the latter were Christian and they did not normally place belongings alongside the dead; in addition, many of the most common objects in Viking graves are of distinctively Scandinavian type. Male graves may contain weapons, horse harness, blacksmith's tools and balance-scales and weights, while female graves may contain a pair of oval brooches, beads, weaving equipment and a sickle (**23**). Both male and female are likely to have knives, whetstones, combs, belt-buckles, brooches and dress-pins, and the brooches and pins were functional rather than purely decorative. A rare example of a child buried alone was found at Valtos in Lewis in 1991, and the only belongings were an amber bead and a stone pendant. The number and quality of the grave-goods are taken to represent the wealth and status in life of the buried person; the position of the objects on and around the body can be useful in reconstructing the clothing which rarely survives and then only as scraps preserved beneath corroding metal. Both woollen and linen textiles were used, with good even weaves.

Viking dress

Scraps of cloth from a tenth-century male grave on the island of Eigg in the Western Isles suggest that he was wearing a cloak of wool with a shaggy pile, a woollen tunic and a linen undergarment, and we may assume some sort of trousers because Scandinavian finds indicate that men wore woollen breeches under their tunics. Female fashion appears to have been as conservative as male, remaining essentially the same throughout the ninth and tenth centuries at least. Women wore a linen shift or chemise, often finely pleated, beneath a woollen pinafore held up by straps fastened with a pair of oval

evidence of boat-burials, two in the Hebrides and two in Orkney. Old excavations can be difficult to interpret, and even where boat-rivets have been recognized in the past they were often not kept and their positions not recorded. The rivets are distinctive: made of iron, they have a rounded head, with a square, rectangular or rhombic washer at the other end (**22**). The washer was secured on the inside of the plank, and the length of the rivet depended upon the thickness of the plank and its position in the structure of the boat. The number of rivets required depended upon the size of the vessel, and even a small boat built of a few planks needed at least fifty rivets, while a larger boat required many more. Several Scottish Viking graves have yielded a small number of rivets, too few to represent a complete boat but perhaps indicating the former presence of a token part of an old boat. In some cases the rivets may have come from a small wooden chest rather from than a boat.

23 *An artist's reconstruction of a wealthy pagan female grave.*

brooches, and a woollen cloak. Footwear was made of leather and consisted of slippers or boots. Long bronze or silver pins are sometimes found beside the heads of female skeletons, suggesting that they wore either elaborate hair-styles or more likely headscarves. We know from the sagas that married women were expected to keep their heads covered.

Brooches and pins and even beads are common to both male and female graves, but oval brooches were strictly female jewellery. The oval brooches seem to have been mass-produced in Scandinavia and dispersed through-out the entire area of Viking influence from Russia in the east to the Atlantic colonies in the west during the ninth and tenth centuries. Sometimes strings of beads were suspended across the chest between the two oval brooches, and useful items such as a knife, whetstone, comb and needle-case might be hung on a cord or fine chain from one of the brooches. Oddly, although silver and gold arm-rings and finger-rings have been found in hoards and as stray

24 *Typical Viking dress for men and women of substance.*

finds in Scotland, none has been found in a grave. There are at least two possible explanations: they were not considered appropriate for burials, or the fashion for wearing them began in the late tenth century in Scotland (pagan burials ceased in the later tenth century at the same time as hoards began to be buried).

Belts were essential for men as a means of carrying a sword as well as knife, whetstone and comb, although the sword could also be carried by a strap over the shoulder. Viking swords were about 0.9m (3ft) long and were designed for slashing rather than stabbing; the blade was made of iron, and the hilt could be highly decorative, sometimes cast in bronze and inlaid with contrasting metals such as silver. The warrior might also be armed with a shield, of which only the central iron boss normally

survives; this protected the hand-grip at the back of the shield, and the rest of the circular shield would be made of wood. Iron spearheads, arrowheads and axes are often found, again lacking the wooden component, the shaft, which rots away (sometimes fragments of wood survive inside the metal socket). Viking axes have a very distinctive shape, almost triangular with a broad cutting edge to the blade. No helmets have been found in Scotland, and only one complete helmet survives in Norway, despite the fact that warriors are shown wearing helmets on contemporary sculpture in England and Sweden. These are simple, rounded helmets with a nose-guard and sometimes eye-and-nose-guards (and definitely no wings or horns as popular modern myth would insist!).

Hoards

'The Hebrideans were so scared of them, they hid whatever they could carry either in among the rocks or underground.' Thus the author of *Orkneyinga Saga* describes the effect that raiding by Vikings from Orkney had on the inhabitants of the Western Isles – and what other way could valuables be kept safe than by burying them? Many such hoards of treasure must have been buried and recovered once the threat had passed, but some remained hidden for centuries, either because their owners failed to return or because their whereabouts were forgotten. The classic example of the problems inherent in burying hoards is the experience of the seventeenth-century English diarist, Samuel Pepys, who relates how, at a time of family crisis, his wife buried all his wealth in the garden. A few months later, when he judged it safe to dig up his valuables, Pepys encountered comical difficulties because his wife could not remember exactly where she had buried them.

Both the Vikings and the native inhabitants were accustomed to burying their most precious belongings in times of trouble, but the hoards can usually be distinguished by the character of their contents. Some thirty hoards of Viking silver have come to light, or at least been recorded, in Scotland, mostly in the Northern and Western Isles, reflecting the major areas of Norse activity and mostly dating to the late tenth and early eleventh centuries. Isolated finds of single gold finger-rings and arm-rings have also been made, but it is impossible to be sure that these were deliberately buried rather than accidentally lost. All such discoveries are made by chance, some during peat-digging, others just by natural processes such as rabbits burrowing or soil erosion bringing the object to the surface where the glint of silver or gold catches the eye.

This makes the known hoards a truly random sample and the pattern of their geographical distribution and dating all the more reliable.

Viking hoards are distinctive because they contain not simply imported silver coins, which also occur in ninth-century native hoards, but hack-silver, ring-money and typically Scandinavian jewellery. Hack-silver is a term used to describe fragments of silver objects which have been chopped up to use simply as bullion, worth only their weight in precious metal. Silver coins were also treated as bullion and often cut into pieces. Ring-money consists of plain silver arm-rings, which were made in multiples of a unit of weight of around 24g (1oz) – the same unit, known as the øre, on which Viking balance-weights were based. These arm-rings were thus a very convenient way of carrying easily measurable wealth on the person. Ring-money first appears in Scotland in the Skaill hoard from Orkney around 950, and continues in use into the eleventh century.

Scotland, the Isle of Man and Ireland

Not surprisingly, there are strong links in Viking Age material culture between Scotland, the Isle of Man and Ireland, despite the fundamental difference in the nature of settlement in Ireland. Scandinavian settlement in Ireland was concentrated in urban trading centres, and considerable wealth can be detected from the great silver hoards that survive. There are comparatively few Scandinavian place-names in Ireland, reflecting the lack of rural settlement. The situation in Man was very similar to that in Scotland, involving warriors from western Norway, but with the difference that they appear not to have taken with them their Norwegian wives. It is as difficult to date precisely the onset of colonization in Man as elsewhere, but it may be that these were the sons of Vikings already settled in the Northern or Western Isles of Scotland rather than newcomers direct from Norway, despite their Norwegian weapons.

Intermarriage between Viking settlers and

native women was one way in which blood became mixed, another was the practice of taking slaves. Slavery was a normal part of life for Vikings, Picts, Scots, Manx and Irish alike, as it was elsewhere in Europe until the twelfth century. Slaves would be a valuable cargo on any scale, but the Norse attack on the British stronghold on Dumbarton Rock in 870 resulted in a massive haul: 'they carried off all the riches that were within it and afterwards a great host of prisoners were brought into captivity', a great host that included Britons, Picts and English, who were taken back to Viking Dublin in a fleet of 200 ships. Many were no doubt set to work in Dublin and others sold to Irish lords. Irish sources tell of Viking cunning in taking advantage of the dark of night or the chaos of storms to mount raids, even attacking great monasteries on festival days when they knew that many people would be gathered together.

The aim in this chapter has been to set the scene for the three chapters that follow, by interpreting in general terms the archaeological evidence that survives in Scotland from the Viking Age proper, the years between about 780 and 1100. The next three chapters will look more closely at what has been found and is now in museums, what can still be seen on the ground and what makes Scotland such a rewarding area in which to explore the Viking achievement.

CHAPTER FOUR

The Viking heartland: the Northern Isles and Caithness

A dramatic discovery was made in Orkney in November 1991. Coastal erosion at Scar in Sanday had revealed human bones, and excavation in the dark winter days uncovered a rich Viking boat-grave set in a stone-lined pit – one side of the boat had been washed away but most of its contents survived for the archaeologists to find (**colour plate 2**). Two days after the excavation was finished, a storm destroyed most of the site. The boat was about 6.3m (21ft) long and had been buried the right way up with three bodies inside it, with a mound piled on top; one end of the boat had been weighted down with large stones and the bodies were placed in the other, western end. The wooden planks had rotted away, but some 300 iron rivets remained in position to outline the shape of the boat.

This was no dragon-ship, rather a rowing boat, far more useful in everyday life among the islands – the sort of traditional small boat still in use along the coast of Norway today. A sample of soil was taken from a point at which two of the wooden planks had overlapped, and analysis revealed the presence of igneous rock particles which are foreign to Orkney. The particles were probably in the caulking that was used to seal the boat during its construction, indicating that the boat had been imported into Orkney, presumably on board a larger vessel.

Buried in the boat were a man, a woman and a child, but the difference in age between the man and the woman suggests that this was not a nuclear family group: while the man was in his thirties, the woman was in her seventies. The child was aged about ten years, but erosion had removed all but the leg bones, together with any belongings. Both adults had rich personal grave-goods, suggesting that they were of equal status rather than master and slave; perhaps some disease killed them or an accident at sea drowned them; we shall never know.

To judge by the grave-goods, these people were buried sometime in the ninth century. The woman and child had been laid on their backs, but the man was in a crouched position with his knees drawn up to his chest, in order to fit him into the narrowing prow of the boat. He was a warrior armed with sword and arrows (there may have been a bow as well but the wood and gut would have perished); the sword was still in its wooden scabbard, which had been lined with sheepskin so that the natural oil in the wool would keep the blade in good condition. He also had a fine bone comb, a lead weight and a set of 22 bone and antler gaming pieces, which were found in a tight pile suggesting that they had been in some sort of leather bag which had perished. The woman was wearing a gilded brooch and beside her were a superbly carved whalebone plaque (**25**), an iron sickle, an iron cooking spit, and a small pair of iron shears and a steatite spindle-whorl, which appeared to have

25 *Whalebone plaque from Scar, Sanday, one of the finest surviving examples of this distinctive Viking artefact.*

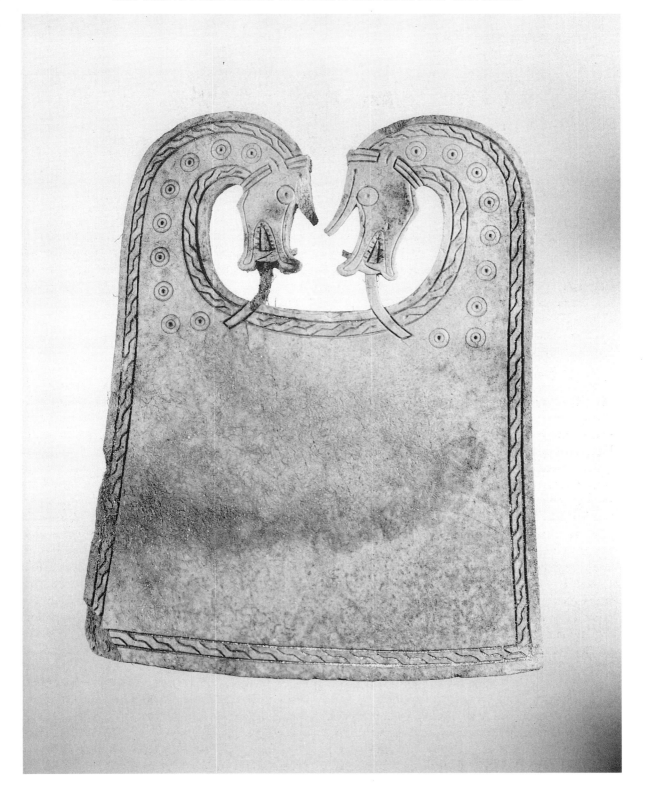

been in a small wooden box. The wood had rotted away but the iron nails survived.

The whalebone plaque from this burial is the only complete example from Scotland and its craftsmanship and design rival the best of those found in Norway. It has a decorative border of key-pattern and, at one end, a pair of graceful horses' or dragons' heads. It has survived in excellent condition – indeed it is barely worn, an odd feature in view of the advanced age of the buried woman. Does it perhaps represent the young wife and mother who is missing from this family group? It is a distinctively Scandinavian artefact of the late eighth to late tenth centuries, and the few found in Scotland were almost certainly brought from Norway in the personal luggage of wealthy settlers. Apart from the Sanday example, fragments of others have been discovered in a possible grave-mound at King's Cross Point on Arran, in a grave at Westness (see below) and in a domestic context at Saevar Howe in Orkney. The Sanday board measures about 280mm (11in) by 200mm (8in) and is

26 *Glass linen smoothers, together with a fragment of a whalebone plaque from King's Cross Point, Isle of Arran.*

15mm ($\frac{1}{2}$in) thick, and it must have been cut from a large rib-bone.

The purpose of these boards is something of a mystery. There are no wear-marks to suggest that they were chopping boards, and their fine decoration implies that they were considered to be of some importance; in Norway they have been found in wealthy women's graves. It has been suggested that they were used in pleating the fine linen cloth worn by well-to-do women, by winding the damp pleated material round the board and leaving it to dry, but a longer board would be more efficient for the task. Perhaps more likely is the idea that they were smoothing boards, particularly if they were used along with the heavy glass objects known as linen smoothers.

These linen smoothers are circular bun-shaped objects of solid dark green-blue glass, usually about 50–70mm (2–2¾in) in diameter, each formed by flattening a single large droplet of glass (26). More than forty have been found in Norway and eleven have been discovered in Scotland, some as stray finds, some from archaeological sites (for instance Gurness and Howe in Orkney) and one at least from a grave (Ballinaby, Islay). The composition of the glass suggests that none should be dated earlier than the tenth century. Their purpose is clear, partly because wear on the convex surface indicates rubbing and partly because identical objects were still in use into the nineteenth century both in Norway and in Scotland. They were used for smoothing linen and in particular for creating a high gloss on white caps for women. Discussing the Ballinaby smoother in 1880, Joseph Anderson was able to refer to the contemporary use of such objects in Norway and to illustrate an example used 'long ago' in a house in Caithness. Some of the later examples have handles, made in one with the smoother, but others are superficially indistinguishable from those of the Viking Age, making the dating of stray finds very difficult. The size of the whalebone plaques would make them very suitable as boards for tasks such as glazing linen caps.

Flax appears to have been introduced as a crop into Orkney in Norse times, for seeds have been identified at the settlements at Pool in Sanday and at Saevar Howe, Birsay. There is some controversy over whether the industry later died out and was reintroduced in the eighteenth century, when it became an important element in the economy. Another tool associated with the manufacture of linen is the heckle, which has long iron spikes designed to strip the flax fibres ready for spinning; the corroded remains of two heckles were found in a ninth-century female grave at Westness, Rousay, Orkney. The same grave yielded another distinctively Scandinavian item of weaving equipment, an iron weaving-batten, which was used to beat the horizontal threads into place on the loom. It consists of a blade and a socket to take a wooden handle, and the iron blade and socket are together about 0.3m (1ft) long (NMS). A second batten was found in another grave at Westness, and parts of two others came from graves in Islay and Barra, but they are more common in Norwegian women's graves.

Viking Sanday

The Scar boat-grave takes pride of place among a number of Viking graves which are known from nineteenth-century discoveries on the north-west coast of Sanday. Several were found on the headland known as Lamba Ness on the west side of Pool Bay, and in recent years a Norse settlement has been excavated on the opposite side of the bay.

Both Sanday and North Ronaldsay are notable for very large mounds known as farm-mounds, some of which have long-established farms built on them while others are simply bare mounds. Place-names indicate both that they existed when the Viking settlers arrived (for instance the Old Norse word, *haugr*, for mound in the farm name How) and that some were chosen as the locations for Viking farms (as in the name Beafield, which is derived from Old Norse *baejar-fjall*, the hill of the farmstead).

One such farm-mound was found to be eroding badly into the sea at Pool, and its contents promised to be rewarding in terms of structures and finds, with the result that a rescue excavation was mounted. Half the mound had already vanished into the sea, leaving a section some 70m (230ft) long and 4m (13ft) high as a slice through prehistory, the classic layer cake in which the debris of centuries has built up to recent times at the top. The build-up began some 5000 years ago with a domestic settlement of stone houses, but occupation was not continuous, for later the site appears to have been abandoned for about two millennia. The next major phase of occupation revealed a substantial roundhouse dating from the fifth century AD. This settlement flourished and new buildings were erected until the early seventh century, after which the community seems to have declined.

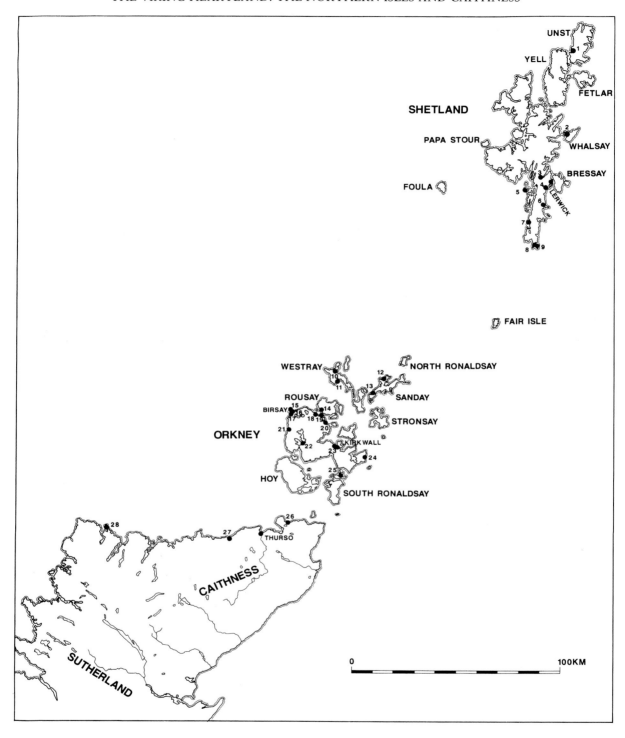

28 *Sub-rectangular house at Pool; the poles mark the positions of post-holes for timber posts to support the roof.*

There were still Picts living here when the Vikings arrived, but their standard of living appears to have deteriorated. It must be remembered, however, that half the site had been destroyed before excavation and that the focus of the Pictish settlement could have been located in the lost area.

The earliest Viking settlers carried out some levelling of the site and built a sub-rectangular house which partially used convenient existing wall-bases; the house had a central hearth but no trace of platforms (28). It has been argued that the idea of platforms or benches was borrowed by the Vikings from native houses, since they are

27 *Map of Viking discoveries in the Northern Isles and northern Scotland mentioned in the text.*
1 *Underhoull;* 2 *Marrister;* 3 *Law Ting Holm;*
4 *Gulberwick;* 5 *Oxna;* 6 *Cunningsburgh;*
7 *St Ninian's Isle;* 8 *Garthsbank;* 9 *Jarlshof;*
10 *Pierowall;* 11 *Tuquoy;* 12 *Scar;* 13 *Pool;*
14 *Westness;* 15 *Brough of Birsay;* 16 *Point of Buckquoy;* 17 *Saevar Howe;* 18 *Burgar;* 19 *Gurness;*
20 *Tingwall;* 21 *Skaill, Deerness;* 22 *Stenness;*
23 *Caldale;* 24 *Skaill;* 25 *Burray;* 26 *Kirk o' Banks;*
27 *Reay;* 28 *Balnakeil.*

not a feature of contemporary houses in Norway, and this evidence from Pool appears to support the argument. The old roundhouse survived in one form or another into the eleventh century, when its walls were finally levelled. Such a well-built structure could clearly be useful, even after its original domestic function had lapsed. The excavator has suggested that there was a continuing native presence during this early Viking phase, perhaps still based in the roundhouse, for the artefacts show a mixture of native and Scandinavian types. The two most notable innovations were steatite vessels and the cultivation of flax.

Viking Rousay

Orkney has been fortunate in the last few decades in the discovery of boat-burials, for two other boats, similar to, though smaller than, that at Scar were found in the cemetery at Westness on the south-west coast of Rousay. Work at this important site came about by chance in 1963 when a farmer dug a pit to bury a cow and discovered a rich Viking grave. The area was already known to have been the scene of Norse activities: Westness or *Vestrnes* is mentioned no fewer than eight times in *Orkneyinga Saga* as the home in the twelfth century of Sigurd, a farmer of some wealth and renown and a friend of Earl Paul Hakonarson. Ploughing in 1826 had turned up a Viking sword and shield-boss, and low mounds in the same field were considered likely to be Viking graves. The grave found in 1963 was closer to the shore, on a low promontory known as Moa Ness, and subsequent fieldwork and excavation have revealed not only a large cemetery on the promontory but also a farm to the north and a boat-house to the south. The topographical relationship between the burials and the settlement is similar to that at Pool but on a smaller and more intimate scale.

The cemetery contained more than thirty graves, some were Viking graves of the ninth century and others were earlier. The latter were burials without grave-goods in stone-lined cists, and radiocarbon dating of the bones suggests that these were native burials of the pre-Norse population spanning perhaps 400 years before the Vikings arrived. The position of these early graves had been marked on the surface by boulders and none was disturbed by grave-digging in Viking times. That such a cemetery should have continued in use carries implications for the relationship between the two peoples (see Chapter 2), and it is to be hoped that one day the pre-Norse, Pictish settlement will be found.

The pagan Viking graves included both boat-burials and oval stone-lined pits, and they contained men, women and children from adults of around fifty years to a newborn infant. The baby was buried with its young mother, presumably as a result of a disastrous birth, and the high quality of her belongings suggests that she was part of a family of some consequence. She

29 *Celtic brooch-pin from Westness; probably made in Ireland around AD 750, this superb cloak-pin was acquired by early Viking settlers in Orkney.*

had a glorious Celtic brooch-pin, the finest of its type ever found, which had probably been made in Ireland about a hundred years before its last owner's death (**29**). Made of silver and gold with insets of amber and red glass, animal heads and intricate filigree decoration, the brooch is a sumptuous masterpiece of the jeweller's craft. The woman also wore a pair of Scandinavian oval brooches, a string of forty beads and a belt or strap with two fine bronze strap-ends. Alongside her were her comb and various items of domestic equipment, including the remains of a bronze bowl, a pair of iron shears, an iron sickle and the whalebone plaque, weaving-batten and iron heckles mentioned already (p.47).

This was not the only wealthy grave in the cemetery. Two boat-graves contained warriors with weapons and tools, one with a sword with an elaborate hilt inlaid with silver. In both cases the boat had been placed upright in a pit, and stones were placed in the prow and stern in order to create a rectangular 'chamber' for the burial. The outlines of the vanished wooden planks were marked by lines of iron rivets, representing boats 5.5m (18ft) and 4.5m (15ft) long, sturdy rowing boats like the Scar boat. In the larger boat, the warrior's shield-boss was so close to his head as to suggest that the entire shield had been placed in the grave first and the warrior laid on top. The boss has a massive dent in it as a reminder of some battle, perhaps the one in which he lost his life. The warrior in the other boat certainly died in battle – the broken blades of four arrowheads were lodged in his body.

An odd feature of the cemetery was a massive stone-setting in the shape of a boat but apparently unfinished. This excavation has yet to be published in detail, and it will add enormously to our understanding both of Viking graves in Scotland and of the people themselves, through analysis of their bones.

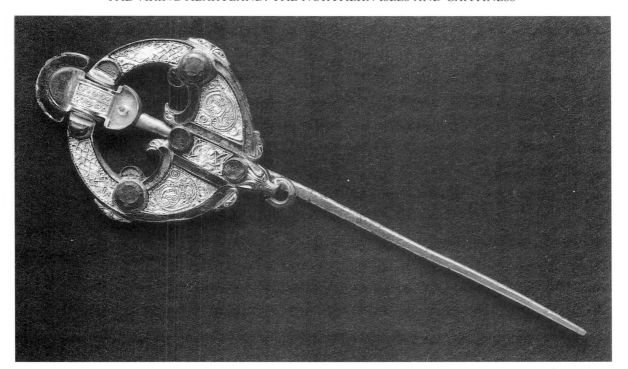

30 *Richly decorated Celtic brooches had a strong appeal for the Vikings: early eighth-century brooch from Hunterston (Ayrshire).*

31 *On the back of the Hunterston brooch is a Viking runic inscription added in the tenth century; it reads 'Melbrigda owns brooch'. Melbrigda or Melbride was a Celtic name, and this man may have been of mixed Celtic and Viking blood.*

If the boat-house, the farm and the cemetery prove to have been contemporary, Westness will present a remarkably rounded picture of a Viking community. The boat-house, or naust as they are known in Orkney, was perfectly located at the head of a gully in the rocky shore, the naust itself dug into the sand and shingle of the shoreline. It was a three-sided stone building, open to the sea; at 4.5m (15ft) wide and more than 8m (26ft) long (there had been some erosion of the seaward end), the naust could easily have accommodated either one large longship or two rowing boats such as those found in the cemetery. Walking from the naust past the cemetery and along the shore, a returning Viking would soon have come to his farm, its buildings arranged, like the naust, end-on to the sea.

The farm consisted of a large dwelling-house and alongside it two byres, one interpreted as a cattle-byre with space for about eighteen animals and the other for sheep. This was a substantial farm, for the dwelling house was almost 35m (115ft) long and 7m (23ft) wide, divided into two large halls with a smaller room between them. The larger hall, 15m (49ft) long, was furnished with low benches along either side of a stone-built hearth. From the animal bones found in the midden, it is clear that pigs were kept as well as cattle and sheep, and analysis of both pollen and burnt grain shows that barley, rye, oats and flax were grown. If cattle and sheep were overwintered indoors in the byres, grass would have had to be cut for hay in the summer. Fishing was concentrated on catching cod and ling, and whales and seals were exploited.

Westness appears at present to be the most complete Viking landscape that we can identify, but there are problems of interpretation: the naust may not belong to the same ninth-century date as the farm and the cemetery, and the excavated farm is neither intact nor likely to have been the only such farm in the vicinity. There is evidence of other graves higher up the slope, and somewhere close lie the remains of Sigurd's establishment. The lower part of a small square tower survives farther north round the

Bay of Swandro from the Viking farm. Known as The Wirk, this has aroused some argument over whether it represents a twelfth-century castle like that in Wyre. The generally accepted opinion, however, is that, along with the massive hall-like building beside it, this belongs to the later Middle Ages. Curiously, discoveries of carved stones have been made near The Wirk and in the walls of the adjacent St Mary's Church, as well as in the grounds of Trumland House to the south, some of which are similar to thirteenth-century sculpture in St Magnus' Cathedral in Kirkwall, while others are of sixteenth-century date.

Mainland Orkney

Probably the most favoured corner of Orkney for settlement from Pictish times onwards was Birsay, the north-west tip of Mainland, and it has certainly been the focus of archaeological activity. In the last century, Kirkwall people took their holidays at Birsay, and bere, a species of barley, was grown here longer than anywhere else in the islands, even today providing enough flour for the special Orcadian bere bannocks. Birsay soils are particularly rich and fertile, nourished by the sand from the Bay of Birsay which consists mostly of ground shell and therefore adds calcium carbonate to the soil when used as a fertilizer. The bay has always been a haven for fishing boats – and seals. Traces of Pictish and Viking settlements have been found round the bay and on the island, the Brough of Birsay, which lies off the tip of the Point of Buckquoy at the north side of the bay (**32**). This small tidal island and the adjacent mainland together seem to have played a special role both in Pictish and in Norse times as a centre of secular and ecclesiastical power. Because of its importance to the Picts, Birsay would have been an obvious target for the earliest Norse settlers as well as for the raiding parties that preceded them (see Chapter 2). Historical references make it clear that Birsay was closely associated with the early Norse earldom.

Viking houses of the ninth century and burials of the tenth century have been excavated both at Saevar Howe at the south end of the bay and on the Point of Buckquoy, and a barn with a corn-drying kiln was uncovered beside the burn in the modern village. None of these sites is visible today, but the extensive Norse remains on the Brough are in State care (**colour plate 3**). The settlements round the bay appear to have been individual farms, but the Brough settlement had a special status which is only partly understood, despite the many seasons of excavation that have taken place there, in the 1930s, the 1950s and the 1970s and 1980s. Unfortunately there has been no publication of the pre-1970s excavations in terms of structures, and these include most of the buildings visible today, although at least the finds have been published (most of which are in RMS but a good selection is in Tankerness House Museum in Kirkwall).

The special status of the site is clear, however, from the number and complexity of the surviv-

32 The Brough of Birsay, Orkney, a tidal island even in Viking times.

ing buildings, and it is tempting to identify this highly defensible settlement with the seat of the earldom in the eleventh century. According to *Orkneyinga Saga*, Earl Thorfinn 'had his permanent residence at Birsay, where he built and dedicated to Christ a fine minster, the seat of the first bishop of Orkney' (chapter 31), but it is not clear whether the Earl's residence or his minster were on the mainland or the island. The phrase used in the saga is 'i Byrgishera∂', which is likely to be a district name equivalent to the later parish of Birsay and Harray (*Byrgisey and Hera∂*), and strong arguments have been put forward to support the location of the minster at least on the mainland – certainly more convenient for the bishop and his congregation. Thorfinn may have maintained a house in mainland Birsay and a retreat on the Brough.

The former has yet to be found but the latter could be identified with a well-built hall and bath-house excavated on the island. It is notoriously difficult, however, to marry in any detail archaeology with the people and events of history, and it is unlikely that this tantalizing problem will ever be resolved.

The island is about 21ha (52 acres) in area, but it slopes up from about 4m (13ft) OD on the east to 45m (148ft) on the west, where there are dramatic cliffs facing the brunt of the Atlantic waves, and settlement was concentrated on the lower slope. It is a tidal island today and there is no reason to suppose that it has not been so for the last two thousand years. There has certainly been coastal erosion and part of the Viking settlement has been lost, but the choice of this location for settlement undoubtedly involved acceptance of the fact that it could only be reached on foot at low tide and by boat at high tide with difficulty. Today's visitor can arrive with dry feet along the concrete causeway, but in Viking times it would be difficult even at low tide to arrive with dignity let alone dry!

The advantage of living on the Brough was its defensibility, and the disadvantages included dependence on the mainland for supplies, inconvenience of access and discomfort: in the winter, salt water bathes the slope and drainage would be an ever-present problem. Nevertheless, there is some reason to believe that climatic conditions were rather easier in the Viking Age than today (see Chapter 1), and the discomfort of living on the Brough less – but not absent, as the elaborate drainage system in the Viking settlement implies. The Brough could never be self-sufficient, for grazing was limited and cultivable land non-existent, and the farms round the bay must have supplied grain and beef at least; one or more of them may have been an official home-farm owned by the Brough estate and charged with supplying its needs. Animal bones recovered in recent excavations on the Brough include both cattle and sheep, and the particular bones suggest that they represent joints of meat rather than complete carcasses, which means that the animals were slaughtered away from the island.

The island community was not, however, entirely dependent upon outside support, for there is evidence of iron-working, essential for the maintenance and replacement of tools and weapons, and the presence of large fishbones and line-sinkers (weights for fishing-lines) indicates that fishing from boats was carried out from the island itself. Steatite moulds for bar ingots imply that more precious metal, such as silver, was on occasion melted down and cast in ingot form.

The visible structures are dominated by the remains of a charming twelfth-century church, but the known occupation of the island spans several centuries from pre-Viking times in the seventh and eighth centuries until the twelfth century, and it remained a place of pilgrimage throughout medieval times. Only the cast of a splendid carved stone and a small well remain to be seen of a substantial Pictish settlement. Norse buildings are scattered over quite a wide area, but unfortunately it is impossible to analyse the development of the entire settlement, even in terms of how many buildings were in use at one time and for what purpose. Certain trends at least can be identified. There are large hall-houses, up to 20m (66ft) or more in length, consisting of living-hall and kitchen separated by nothing more than a wooden screen, smaller buildings which may have been outhouses, and complexes of walls representing modification and rebuilding over a long period.

As at Jarlshof (see below), the hall-house and separate outhouse was the primary design, and later a nucleated design was adopted in which additional rooms were built on to the sides of the main house. Missing from the Brough of Birsay is the true longhouse, in which a byre was added to one end of the dwelling house, for this type of building was irrelevant to an island dependent

33 *Early Viking houses on the Brough of Birsay.*
34 *Later Viking houses on the Brough of Birsay.*

35 *Possible bath-house on the Brough of Birsay.*

upon the mainland for animal husbandry. On the easternmost tip of the island are the eroded remains of a very large hall-house and a small specialized building which may have been a bath-house or sauna: it has a central hearth and benches and a drain lining the walls (35). On the edge of the cliff at the northern end of the settlement is a blacksmith's workshop, identified from the remains of a smelting hearth and iron slag.

The artefacts from the early Norse levels include both native and Scandinavian types: native bone pins and combs and a bronze penannular brooch; Scandinavian bone combs (36) and needle-cases (37), a bone weaving tablet for making decorative braid, steatite spindle-whorls and a seal's tooth pendant inscribed with runes (38). The root end of the tooth is perforated and lightly incised with the first six letters of the runic alphabet, probably as a protective charm. There are also three bronze dress-pins of

Irish manufacture (39). The preservation of iron was not good but it is clear that it was used extensively for many items from knives to nails and buckles. Whetstones were more common than the blades they sharpened.

The finds from later levels are not as rich as might have been hoped from a high-status site such as this, but the buildings had clearly been kept clean and there were no extensive midden deposits – these may have been on the lower perimeter of the site, long vanished into the sea. Fashions in hair-combs changed with time, from the long hogbacked combs of the ninth century to smaller combs kept in matching bone cases (40) and thence to combs with high backs and tiny bronze rivets which were both functional and decorative. Long bone and bronze dress- or hair-pins suited Viking taste, and a neat bronze

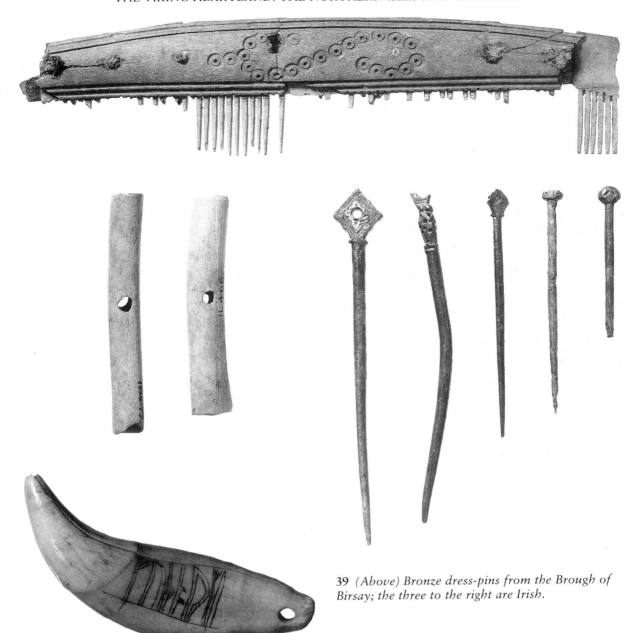

39 (Above) Bronze dress-pins from the Brough of
Birsay; the three to the right are Irish.

36 (Top) Early Norse bone comb from the Brough
of Birsay.

37 (Middle left) Bone needle-cases from the Brough
of Birsay.

38 (Bottom left) Seal's tooth pendant inscribed
with runes from the Brough of Birsay.

strap-end has an animal-head at either end (41); a few coloured glass beads point to the strings of beads worn by pagan Viking women in death. These are good reminders that, on the whole, we should not expect to find many expensive personal belongings lying about on domestic sites: they would be handed down or melted down or exchanged for bags of grain or sides of beef.

Excavations in the 1970s and 1980s were

occupying the same plots of land, and dating evidence indicated that the Viking takeover of the island occurred in the late eighth or early ninth century. There was also evidence of a controlling authority over the Viking community: a major phase of building took place in the later ninth century, around the time of the establishment of the earldom of Orkney, and the houses were all aligned in the same direction and protected by a common drainage system. Some-

40 *Bone comb-case from the Brough of Birsay.*

41 *Bronze strap-end from the Brough of Birsay.*

42 *Bone line-stretcher, perhaps used on boat-rigging, from the Brough of Birsay.*

largely concerned with areas along the very edge of the island where structures were suffering from coastal erosion to north and south of the main site (which is protected by a concrete sea-wall), including the precipitous finger of land known as 'the Peerie Brough', the little Brough. The area immediately to the south of the main site produced particularly interesting results: the layout of the primary Viking settlement conformed to the earlier Pictish layout, the houses time in the late tenth or early eleventh century, the drainage system was obliterated, the land levelled and new buildings on a new common alignment were erected. The special status of the Brough of Birsay during both Pictish and Viking times is inescapable, as is its connection with the seat of the earldom in the late ninth, tenth and eleventh centuries.

Perhaps surprisingly, the only identifiable thing-site, the place of assembly where judicial matters were settled, is not at Birsay but in Rendall on the north-east coast of Mainland, where its location is indicated by the place-name Tingwall (from Old Norse *thing-vollr*, assembly field or enclosure). It is, however, central to a wide area of early Viking settlement, whereas Birsay was on the perimeter. Viking activity in the immediate vicinity of Tingwall includes a ninth-century female grave dug into the ruins of the old broch at Gurness. Buried in a slab-lined long cist (**43**), the woman was wearing a pair of bronze oval brooches (**44**) and an iron necklet, and beside her were an iron knife and an iron sickle. There may have been other graves disturbed in more recent times, for several Scandinavian objects were found high up in the great mound covering the broch settlement.

43 *Sketch plan of a pagan female Viking burial at Gurness, drawn at the time of excavation in 1939; the positions of the two oval brooches show that they were worn just below the shoulders.*

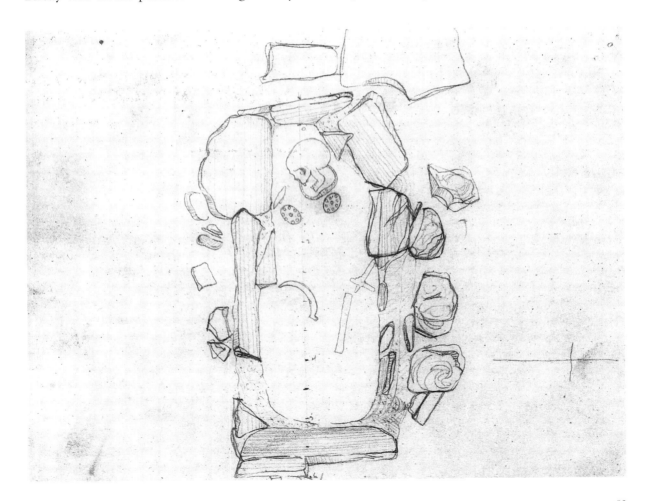

44 *Oval brooch from the female grave at Gurness; cast in bronze, these typically Scandinavian brooches have been found throughout the Viking world.*

These were objects more commonly found as grave-goods than as strays: two iron shield-bosses, a glass linen smoother and a bronze folding balance. North along the coast from Gurness, exploration of another great broch-mound at Burgar, in the nineteenth century, yielded not only a hoard of superb Pictish silver and amber but also two gold arm-rings of Viking date.

Another site where Viking settlement replaced a flourishing Pictish settlement is Skaill in Deerness, which has been identified as the residence of Thorkel Amundason, foster-father to Earl Thorfinn in the early eleventh century (*Orkneyinga Saga*, chapter 14). It is not known whether the estate belonged to Thorkel's family two centuries earlier at the time of the primary settlement. The excavated site is incomplete, for coastal erosion had destroyed part of it and modern farm buildings overlie it (**45**). On the surviving evidence, the ninth-century buildings were of poor quality, and there appears to have been a period of abandonment in the later ninth and possibly early tenth centuries, unless the focus of settlement at that time lay to the eroded east. The details of the excavation have yet to be published. The place-name Skaill has two meanings, for the Old Norse word 'skali' can mean

either hall or hut, but in Orkney it survives as a farm name in the best locations and seems to indicate settlements of high status. There was certainly a splendid medieval church here, a 'steeple-kirk' with twin round towers, which was demolished in order to build the present church, and a fine hogback tombstone of the late eleventh or early twelfth century survives as a reminder of the older church (see p.109). Part of an early Christian cross-slab was found reused as a paving-stone in the Viking settlement.

There ought to be a substantial Viking settlement somewhere in the vicinity of Pierowall in Westray, to account for the cemetery discovered in the sand-dunes to the north of the modern village in the nineteenth century. At least seventeen graves were found but there were probably more, and some were of high status. The records are scanty but three burials were accompanied by a horse and one by both a horse and a dog, and there was clearly a variety of grave structures and rituals. In one case the skull may have been cleft, perhaps the victim of some battle. References to Westray in *Orkneyinga Saga* are frequent and the Viking Age population of the island must have been substantial, but the only settlement located to date is at Tuquoy on the west coast (see Chapter 7).

Scandinavian place-names in the Northern Isles

Orkney and Shetland are comparatively rich in archaeological remains of the Viking Age, yet even here the evidence of the sagas and of place-names shows how vast must be the body of untraced remains. Scandinavian place-names obliterated all but a handful of indigenous names, and they cover not simply farm-names and the more obvious landscape features but also every nook and cranny round the coast, vital to seafarers and fishermen. As already noted, many names correspond to names in Norway and are useful indicators of the origin of the Viking settlers, but they are not simply com-

45 *Aerial view of excavations at Skaill in 1965; Norse buildings are visible in the foreground and to the left of the farm.*

memorative in the sense of naming the new land after the old. Many names were used because they were appropriate: Old Norse *Sandvik*, modern Sandwick, was applied to many a sandy bay, while *Leirvik*, Lerwick, was probably another literal name, mud bay, rather than named after one particular Leirvik in the homeland.

Shetland

We ought to know far more about Viking Shetland than we do, but only now is the landscape being examined by archaeologists in the detail that it deserves. Late Norse Shetland has fared better, with excavations on Papa Stour and Unst (see Chapter 7), but understanding of the period before 1100 depends too heavily on the site at Jarlshof. Plenty of potential Viking sites are scattered across this largely undeveloped landscape, but a concentrated campaign of fieldwork and excavation is needed to confirm their Viking origin. At present only two settlements are known, at the southern extremity of Shetland at Jarlshof and at the northern extremity at Underhoull on Unst, and there have been no excavations of Viking Age sites apart from the steatite workings at Cunningsburgh for more than twenty years. Current studies of the ancient steatite industry promise exciting results.

Cunningsburgh

Apart from fishing, the most important natural resource in Shetland at this period was steatite – a soft rock, also known as soapstone, which is largely composed of talc and can be carved easily with metal tools. Steatite outcrops occur in a number of places in mainland Shetland, Fetlar and Unst, but the major workings to have been identified and studied are those at Cunningsburgh, south of Lerwick, and at Clibberswick on the east coast of Unst.

Cunningsburgh has a most interesting history. Its Old Norse name means king's stronghold, and it is likely that this name was given in recognition of the status of this area as a centre of Pictish power in Shetland. There are extensive steatite workings on either side of the Catpund Burn, and the exploitation of this covetable resource would have made the landowner a very wealthy man. Wealth brings power and patronage, and it seems likely that Cunningsburgh was part of the estate of a Pictish secular ruler, perhaps the regional king for Shetland. There is tangible support for this idea in the discovery at Mail on the Cunningsburgh coast of three ogam inscriptions and a remarkable carving of a wolf-headed figure dressed in a tunic and carrying an axe and a club. The figure must relate to Pictish pagan religion, perhaps a shaman wearing a mask or, as kings in early religions were often seen as personifications of gods, a portrait of a god-king. Three Norse runic inscriptions have also been found at Mail, including one of the earliest in the Northern Isles, suggesting along with the Norse place-name that this Pictish power-centre was taken over by the Norse at an early stage in their settlement – another politically adroit move comparable to the takeover of Birsay in Orkney. None of the inscriptions is complete but they appear to be memorial in

46 *Steatite bowls from Jarlshof.*

intent: the early inscription ends '... *aftir fothur sinn Thorbiorn*', '... after his/her father Thorbiorn'.

Steatite was used for a wide range of artefacts and was already familiar to the Vikings in their homeland, for Norway has many outcrops of this useful rock, particularly in Hordaland. The Norse name for steatite was *kleberg* which means 'loomweight stone' and reflects one of the most common objects for which it was used. Open-cast quarrying was used at Cunningsburgh, and many clear traces of the bowls cut from the rock-surface can still be seen amongst the workings on either side of the Catpund Burn (**colour plate 5**).

The technique used was to carve the outside of the bowl upside down and protruding from the rockface, then to sever it from the rock and finally to hollow out the interior and smooth down the surfaces. To judge from the sequence at Jarlshof, different shapes of vessel were popular at different times: round, oval, square or rectangular (**46**). Steatite was also used to make line-sinkers for fishing (**47**), trough-like dishes, lamps, thin flat discs which were used as baking plates or griddles, spindle-whorls and other equipment.

Jarlshof

Jarlshof owes its romantic name to Sir Walter Scott, who visited Sumburgh during his tour with the Northern Lighthouse Board in 1814 and later set there the opening scene of his novel, *The Pirate*. All that was visible then were the ruins of

47 *Steatite line-sinkers for weighting fishing-lines, Brough of Birsay.*

48 *The sixteenth-century laird's house at Jarlshof, with Sumburgh Head in the distance.*

the seventeenth-century laird's house (48), and it was this that Sir Walter named Jarlshof or 'Earl's Mansion', suggesting that 'an ancient Earl of the Orkneys had selected this neck of land for establishing a mansion-house'; he would be gratified to know that excavations more than a century later proved that there had indeed been Viking Age settlement here, long before the laird's house was built.

We cannot know the name by which the Norsemen knew this settlement, for it is not identified in *Orkneyinga Saga*; the composer of the saga seems to have been little interested in Shetland, and only mentions specific Shetlanders when listing the miracles attributed to St Magnus. The name by which this whole promontory is known, Sumburgh, comes from the Old Norse name, *Svinaborg*, meaning either 'Svein's fort' or 'the fort of the pigs'. The fort may refer to the old broch at Jarlshof, which would still have been visible and may even have been defensible at the

time of the Norse settlement. Svein could be the first Norse colonist to take over the site – or perhaps the early Norse settlers used 'pigs' as a derogatory term for the native population.

The site at Jarlshof had attracted settlement from early prehistoric times, resulting in a very long archaeological sequence which began probably in the late third millennium BC and continued, though not necessarily in an unbroken sequence, to the laird's house of the seventeenth century AD (**colour plate 6**). Unfortunately, the immediately pre-Norse period seems to have witnessed a lull in the occupation of the site, but that will have made the Norse takeover easier. The site was first discovered in the late nineteenth century after storm damage to the shore revealed massive stone walls belong-

1 The western seaways; Sorisdale on the island of Coll.

2 Boat-burial at Scar, Sanday, Orkney; yellow markers show the position of the rivets.

3 Aerial view of the Viking settlement on the Brough of Birsay, Orkney.

4 *(Top right)* A hoard of Viking gold finger-rings from Stenness, Orkney.

5 *(Bottom right)* Steatite quarry at Cunningsburgh, Shetland; both round and square vessels have been carved from the rock-face.

6 Aerial view of Jarlshof, Shetland; the Norse houses are to the left, and the white gravel floor of the first farmhouse stands out.

7 *(Above)* A classic location for a Viking farm; the farm at Underhoull, Shetland, lies on the far slope above the sheltered bay.

8 *(Right)* Hogback tombstone on the island of Inchcolm in the Firth of Forth.

9 *(Below)* St Magnus' Church, Egilsay.

10 *(Right)* St Magnus' Cathedral, Kirkwall.

11 Runic inscriptions in the chamber of Maes Howe, Orkney; illustration from the original 1862 publication.

12 The festival of Up-Helly-Aa, Lerwick, Shetland; the boat is set ablaze.

49 *The Norse settlement at Jarlshof.*

ing to the prehistoric settlement; the landowner carried out some excavation with promising results and the site was taken into the care of the State in 1925.

Jarlshof has seen intensive bouts of excavation in the twentieth century, with the result that its sequence tends to dominate Shetland archaeology, but the immense problems of digging a multi-period site over several decades have inevitably blurred the details of its stratigraphy. Nor should its entire sequence be taken as typical for Shetland as a whole: the overall picture of the Norse settlement is acceptable, but the pre-Norse hiatus must be local. Pictish Jarlshof is minimal, yet discoveries elsewhere in the islands imply that there was a thriving community in the eighth and ninth centuries, and the conclusion must be that Jarlshof is not typical of this period and that there have been too few excavations elsewhere to balance the evidence from Jarlshof. It is also possible that the focus of the Pictish settlement lay to the seaward side of the broch complex and has been lost into the sea.

The location of the site had been carefully chosen by its prehistoric founders, lying on good fertile land on the well-drained lower slopes of the sandstone promontory of Sumburgh Head, close to the sheltered waters of the West Voe with access to the sea both from there and, a short distance to the north-east, from Gruting Voe on the east coast of the peninsula. There are freshwater springs nearby and an endless supply of building stone on the beach.

The mass of walls belonging to the Viking settlement gives the misleading impression that Jarlshof must have been a small hamlet, but these are the superimposed walls of buildings erected, modified and levelled over several centuries. Jarlshof was never more than a farm, although it grew more substantial as the years went by and the family increased in size. The process of rebuilding on one spot over such a long period makes dating individual structures very difficult, because the layers of soil have been cut into and soil moved from one place to another, with the result that datable objects have become mixed up. The building sequence can be

established through the physical relationship of one wall to another, but the detailed chronology of Jarlshof remains unclear. The first farm is likely to have been established some time in the ninth century, because a gilt bronze harness-mount made in Ireland in the eighth or ninth century was found in the earliest building-levels.

The early Norse settlers built their farmhouse close to the ruins of the old broch, sturdily designed some eight or nine hundred years earlier and doubtless a handy source of good stone. The Viking farmhouse was a simple long rectangular house (**cover**), with one long wall slightly bowed and two opposing entrances (a clever device which meant that whichever door was out of the wind could be used, to avoid draughts). The bowing is no more than an irregularity in the building, and there is no evidence here of boat-shaped houses. The original length of the house is uncertain, owing to the fact that its east gable-wall was later demolished

50 *An artist's reconstruction of the first farmhouse at Jarlshof.*

in order to add on a byre, but the floor-area inside is likely to have been about 22 by 5m (72 by 16ft) (**50**).

There were two rows of wooden posts helping to support the roof and two extra posts at the east end to lend additional support to the hipped roof (these extra posts are sometimes taken as evidence that the house had a timber gable but this is unlikely). The walls were built of stone with an earthen core, and there was some evidence on the north wall of alternate courses of stone and turf having been used for the outer wall-face, perhaps a rebuilding which would account for its bowed appearance. Inside, the house was divided into two on the line of the two doorways, creating a large living-hall to the east and a small kitchen to the west, and there is likely to have been a wooden partition between the two. In the living-hall, there was a raised wooden platform along each wall, which would have been used for seating as well as sleeping and as a working space, and a large central hearth. The two rows of posts supporting the roof ran along the inner edge of the platforms. The kitchen was furnished both with a central hearth and an oven built into the end-wall. Apart from its supporting posts, no evidence survived of the roof, but it is likely to have been timber-framed with a main ridge, covered with turf.

Other buildings included a rectangular barn or byre, and two smaller buildings which have been interpreted as a smithy and a bath-house: the hearth in the 'smithy' contained many fragments of iron clinker, while the 'bath-house' had a large and carefully built hearth suggesting that water may have been thrown on hot stones to create a sauna. An alternative use for the latter building may have been the essential drying of grain.

After some time, the 'bath-house' went out of use and two new outhouses were erected, one of which had a cobbled floor and may have been a stable. A wall running northwards from the original farmhouse has been interpreted as part of another dwelling but cannot certainly be identified as such, though in time other buildings including dwellings were built north of and at right angles to the first farmhouse. The pattern of separate dwelling-house and outbuildings appears to have been replaced, perhaps in the eleventh century, by the true longhouse in which humans and animals were housed under one roof. Both the original dwelling and a later dwelling were modified in this way. The original farmhouse was lengthened by demolishing the east end-wall and adding a byre with paving down the central area and an entrance in the gable, served by a narrow paved passage (51). The passage would funnel the animals one by one into the byre. The house is now displayed with a white gravel floor, making it easier for the visitor to distinguish its design.

Later still, in the twelfth and thirteenth centuries, the design of the dwellings was modified again: instead of a simple linear plan with kitchen, living-hall and byre in line in one long building, additional space was achieved by building rooms on to the long walls of the original house (52). This broad pattern of architectural development seems to hold good throughout the Norse Atlantic colonies. The first farmhouse at Jarlshof appears to have been used and modified over a period of almost two hundred years; even after it was finally abandoned, one end of it was converted into an outhouse. This was common practice into the twentieth century: old dwellings became barns after the new house was built, and the two can often be seen side by side, the contrast particularly vivid in the Western Isles where the new bungalow stands beside the old blackhouse.

The years of excavation at Jarlshof produced a wide variety of artefacts, both everyday equipment and more exotic items (mostly in NMS but some are in the site museum and some in the Shetland Museum in Lerwick). The steatite bowls have already been mentioned, and other objects were also carved from this useful rock: hanging lamps in which the wick floated in a pool of oil; line-sinkers for fishing; loom-weights and spindle-whorls; beads and even a tiny bowl and a miniature quern which were probably toys. Bone and antler were used to make dress-pins, hair combs, toggles, needle cases, handles for iron knives, awls, door-snecks and other domestic equipment. An unusual item is a sliver of bone with a hole at either end, interpreted as a bit for a lamb's mouth to prevent it from sucking all its mother's milk (what remained could then be used for the human family). Combs were normally highly decorated and sometimes pins and handles were also skilfully carved: four sturdy dress-pins have amusingly sculpted animal heads (53).

The local sandstone provided not simply building material but a host of other objects from weights to querns. Whetstones were essential equipment for sharpening iron knives and sickle blades – swords and spearheads too, but the only weapon found was a spearhead. Metal

52 *(Above) A late Norse house at Jarlshof with additional rooms built on to the left side.*

objects other than iron are rare, not necessarily because the family could not afford bronze and silver but because both can be melted down and reused. The loss of a piece of silver ring-money (see below) must have been a severe blow to its owner: it was found in a tenth-century drain. Fine bronze dress-pins and a highly ornamented horse harness-mount are likely to have been imports from Scotland or Ireland, while a strap-end decorated in typical Scandinavian style must surely have been a gift from the homeland. The few glass beads, and one of rock-crystal, also rank as imports.

51 *(Left) The original farmhouse at Jarlshof was converted into a longhouse by the addition of a byre and an entrance passage at one end.*

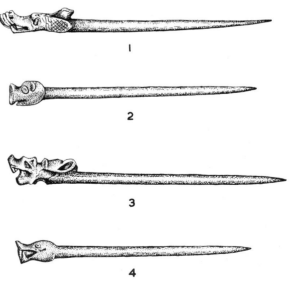

53 *Bone pins with animal heads from Jarlshof.*

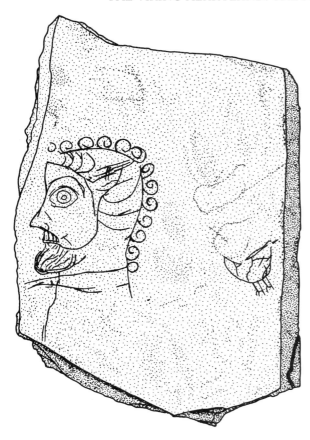

55 *Three Pictish warriors on the symbol stone from the Brough of Birsay; their oval eyes are very similar to the Jarlshof portrait, and the leading warrior has the same curls of hair.*

54 *Portrait of a young man from Jarlshof; found in the early Norse levels, this is probably the work of a Pictish artist.*

Unique to Jarlshof is a series of graffiti scratched on to pieces of slate and sandstone, most of little artistic merit but some remarkable for a sure and economical hand. Two are portraits in profile of a young man (54) and an old man, two are drawings of boats, and others include a four-legged animal and interlace decoration. On the grounds that they were found in Viking levels, these graffiti have been assumed to be Viking in origin, but the style of carving is Pictish – the young man, for example, is almost identical to the warriors on the Pictish symbol stone from Brough of Birsay in Orkney (55) – and a Pictish origin is more plausible. They may perhaps be pre-Viking objects that have been re-deposited in Viking levels, or they may be the work of a Pict taken as a slave. Perhaps the most important question is this: are the boats Viking or Pictish (56)?

At no time at Jarlshof were there more than two dwelling-houses in use, underlining the fact that this was the home of a single extended family. The longevity of the farm demonstrates its success as an economic unit. Sheep, cattle and pigs were bred for their meat, milk, skins and bone, and there were a few ponies of small size but larger than the modern Shetland pony. The remains of a single dog were found, probably a terrier. The carcasses of seals and whales were utilized, and a wide variety of bird bones included both domestic and wild species. Deep-sea fishing brought in very large fish, the heads alone often 300mm (12in) long. Cod, saithe and ling were eaten, probably along with smaller fish whose bones were too small to be recovered without sieving the soil. Charcoal from the middens indicates that hazel, birch and willow grew in the vicinity, probably as pockets of light scrub, and that pine and oak were available either as driftwood or as imported timber.

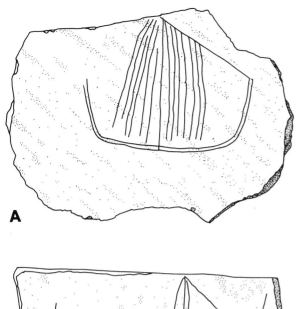

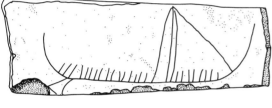

56 *Sketches of boats from Jarlshof – are they of Pictish or Viking vessels?*

For a while, the discovery of the horn of a North American sheep seemed to promise exciting proof of connections between Jarlshof and the New World. In 1941 a German aircraft had dropped a bomb to the north of the Viking houses, and the horn was found in the sand thrown out of the crater. Alas, excavation ten years later uncovered the remains of a nineteenth-century fisherman's bothy, making it more likely that this large horn was a souvenir of a fishing trip.

Viking Tingwall

Best known today for its airfield, Tingwall was an important administrative and judicial centre in Norse times. As already noted, the name

Tingwall means assembly field or enclosure, and this is the most impressive and comprehensible site in Scotland for a Norse lawthing. The Loch of Tingwall lies inland from the sea in the central belt of mainland Shetland between Lerwick and Scalloway, surrounded by some of the most fertile farmland in Shetland with access to fresh water supplies, some woodland, peat and limestone for building material. A small promontory known as Law Ting Holm projects into the loch from its northern end, and traces are visible of a stone-built causeway leading out to a stone enclosure which is likely to have been the meeting-place for the annual Shetland Lawthing or parliament. There are historical references to the lawthing meeting here in 1307 and it was still in use as late as the sixteenth century.

Viking Unst

The northernmost island of the Shetland group ought to have been a vital staging post on the seaway between the Celtic west, the Northern Isles, Norway, the Faeroes and Iceland, and we should expect to find evidence of Viking Age settlement here. Archaeological exploration has been limited, but there are visible sites possibly of Viking age, and proven Norse activity at the steatite outcrops at Clibberswick on the east coast and a settlement at Underhoull on the west coast. Yet another example of a Norse site established literally on top of an earlier native settlement, this is a classic location close to a sheltered bay in which boats could be landed, and from which the resources of the sea could be exploited (**colour plate 7**). Close by was land suitable both for grazing and cultivation, and there was access to steatite outcrops for the manufacture of domestic equipment.

Still visible here on the slope below a ruined broch are the foundations of a hall-house, with paved pathways leading to its entrances and two secondary outhouses added on to one long wall. The excavator interpreted one end of the building as a byre, but there are no positive signs of such a use apart from a partially paved floor which can have other functions. Also, the fact that this was the higher end of the building would make such a design unwise. There was no good dating evidence and occupation at any time in the ninth to eleventh centuries is possible. Despite the apparent advantages of its location, this was not a successful settlement, for there is no sign of growth and, although the house was in use long enough to require repair and modification, its life was relatively short.

Viking Fair Isle

A vital staging post on the long and treacherous voyage between Orkney and Shetland, Fair Isle bears an Old Norse name, *Friðarey*, meaning 'peaceful isle', and it is mentioned several times in *Orkneyinga Saga*. In chapter 56 we are told that a farmer named Dagfinn lived on the island, in chapter 66 that a beacon was set alight there to act as warning of attack from the rival earl in Shetland, with another beacon on North Ronaldsay and other islands, and in chapter 67 we learn more about Dagfinn Hlodvisson of Friðarey, 'a stouthearted farmer' who was charged with 'the task of guarding the beacon there and setting fire to it if the enemy fleet were seen approaching from Shetland'. Although an archaeological survey has been carried out on Fair Isle, nothing has been found which can be dated to this period or even point to a site that might prove useful in tracing Viking Age remains.

Caithness

The name Caithness derives from Old Norse, *Katanes*, meaning 'headland of the cats', and it is assumed that the pre-Norse inhabitants of the area had 'cats' as a tribal name or at least were so called by their neighbours. The land to west and south the Norsemen called *Suðreland*, Southland (Sutherland), just as they called the Hebrides the South Isles, *Suðreyjar*, both being south from the point of view of people settled in the Northern Isles and the far north of mainland Scotland. In return, the Gaelic-speakers of Sutherland referred to Caithness as *Gallaibh* or 'among the strangers', and the Hebrides were known as *Innse Gall*, 'Islands of the Strangers', in both cases the strangers being the Norsemen. Place-names in Caithness suggest that Norse settlement here was somewhat later, perhaps a couple of generations later, than in the Northern Isles: early names incorporating *staðir* are absent, but there are plenty of *bolstaðir* names, as in Scrabster and Lybster.

Archaeological evidence seems to tell the same story, for none of the pagan graves need be earlier than the tenth century and the few known domestic sites date even later, to the late Norse period. The archaeological sample is, however, small and may be heavily biased, and future work may well reconstruct a different picture; most of the archaeological evidence at present comes from along the east coast, whereas Scandinavian place-names extend westwards into the Caithness interior. A small cemetery existed on the north coast at Reay on Sandside Bay to the west of Thurso, and there should be a settlement in the vicinity: at least five graves were found as a result of sand-dune erosion in the early twentieth century.

A few Scandinavian objects have been found in the Golspie area of eastern Sutherland, and these may well represent graves which were not recognized as such at the time. Until recently the northern coast of Sutherland was oddly blank on any map of Viking finds, despite the frequency with which Viking boats must have passed on their way between the Northern and Western Isles. One dot can now be added to the map, for an important male grave was discovered in 1992 at Balnakeil, near Durness.

Hoards in Orkney, Shetland and Caithness

The largest hoard of Scandinavian silver was discovered in Orkney in 1858. A boy was walking across the sand-dunes at the north end of Skaill Bay on the west coast when he noticed

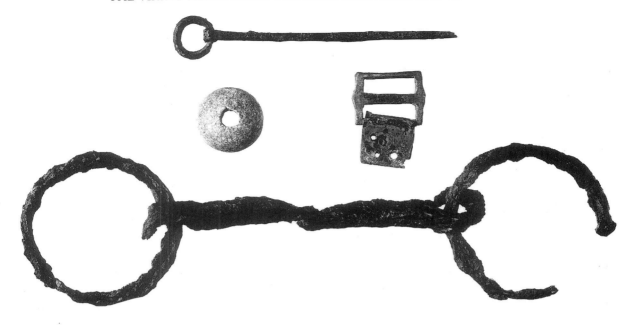

57 *Grave-goods from a female grave at Reay; a bronze ring-pin; a steatite spindle-whorl; a bronze buckle and an iron horse-bit.*

the glint of metal amongst the earth at the entrance to a rabbit-burrow, and his finds, together with those made later by other people at the same spot, add up to a treasure of well over 7kg (15lb) of silver. Given that some items were probably not found and others not given up to the authorities, the original treasure was probably 8kg (18lb) or more in weight and would equal the largest hoards found in Scandinavia itself. The presence of Arabic coins, none of which is later in date than the 940s, indicates that the hoard was buried around 950, perhaps during some major power-struggle, or perhaps simply while its owner was elsewhere on a journey from which he or she failed to return. There ought to be an important Norse settlement in the vicinity, but none has yet been found, although a pagan male grave was found at the south end of the bay. The sea has scoured out Skaill Bay ever larger over the centuries, and a settlement close to the shore in the tenth century may well have been lost through more recent coastal erosion.

The hoard consists of more than one hundred objects, including neck-rings, armlets, brooches, pins, coins, ingots and fragments of silver. Now, more than a thousand years later, it is difficult to know whether this was simply family wealth or the accumulated silver of a merchant or perhaps both; the hack-silver or fragmentary silver indicates that metal had been cut up to meet whatever measures were needed, and the ingots probably represent old silver melted down for reuse, and either could have been required in the course of trade or for paying off a warband. There are 36 complete or fragmentary examples of the type of plain silver armlet known to us as 'ring-money' (see p.42), again an artefact which would be at home in either context.

The most startling objects in the hoard are the thistle-brooches (59). These are huge penannular brooches surely designed for male use and probably worn only on special occasions: for example, one is almost 170mm (7in) in diameter and its pin almost 400mm (16in) long, lethal to an unwary embrace! These brooches have been termed 'thistle-brooches' on account of the great thistle-shaped terminals to the hoop of the

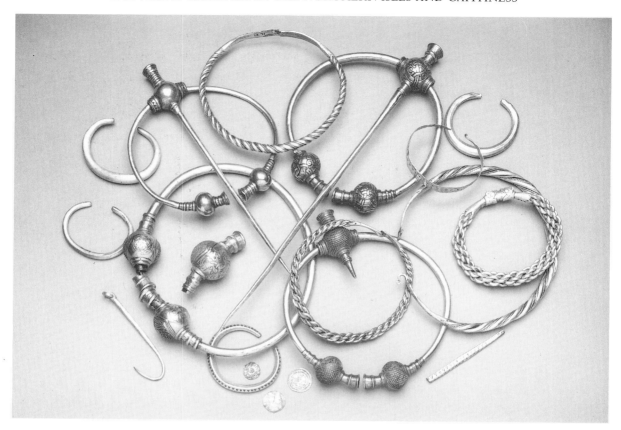

brooch and head of the pin. The 'thistles' presented an ideal surface for decoration, and they are incised with interlaced animals in typical Scandinavian style; the ornament on all the brooches is so similar that they are likely all to have been created by one craftsman. Moreover, the ornament is very close in design to the animal ornament on some of the Isle of Man stone crosses, suggesting not only that the craftsman may have been trained somewhere in the area around the Irish Sea but also that he had been subject to Christian influence.

'Thistle-brooches' are a special variety of the 'ball-type' of penannular brooch which has ball-shaped terminals and which has been found throughout the Viking world from Iceland to Russia. A bronze copy of a silver 'ball-brooch' was found with a male burial at Kildonan on the western island of Eigg. It was probably made in Norway where bronze and iron versions were

58 Part of the great hoard of Viking silver from Skaill, buried around AD 950; the small plain arm-rings on the left are typical examples of ring-money.

common in the tenth century. The 'ball-type' brooch seems to have been developed by Irish craftsmen in the late ninth century and to have been adopted by Scandinavian workshops, another example of the way in which the chameleon Vikings were quick to take up good ideas from the native people in the areas they colonized.

Orkney has yielded another large hoard of Viking silver, some 1.9 kg (4lb) in weight, from the island of Burray. It was found in 1889 during peat-cutting at the north end of the island, when the digger's spade struck a wooden bowl containing 26 armlets or ring-money, 110 fragments

59 *A silver thistle-brooch from the Skaill hoard.*

of ring-money, one complete neck-ring and fragments of another, one complete and one fragment of silver ingot, and three Anglo-Saxon coins which indicate that the hoard was buried around the turn of the tenth century. Only small fragments of the wooden bowl have survived unfortunately, for it would have been an interesting example of a class of artefact which must have been very common but about which we know very little.

Apart from those in the Skaill hoard, one other silver thistle-brooch has been found in Scotland, a chance find from Gulberwick south of Lerwick in Shetland; it is said to have been found by a small boy who was about to melt it down for fishing leads when his father intervened. Other such single discoveries in Shetland include a gold armlet from Oxna and a gold finger-ring from Marrister in Whalsay, both made by twisting together thin gold rods. A

hoard of silver was found at Garthsbank, near Quendale, in 1830 and consisted of six or seven armlets or ring-money and a horn filled with Anglo-Saxon silver coins, the dates of which indicate that the hoard was buried around 1000. This hoard is now lost, as is a very similar hoard from Caldale near Kirkwall in Orkney, again consisting of ring-money and a horn full of coins; it also appears from the coins to have been buried in the early eleventh century. From a field near the shore of the Loch of Stenness in Orkney came a hoard of four gold finger-rings, two made as plain penannular rings and two made of fine rods twisted and plaited together (**colour plate 4**).

The only hoard found to date in Caithness consisted solely of ring-money and its find-spot is especially interesting. Some workmen were cutting a drain through an ancient church site in 1872; this was Kirk o'Banks beside the mouth of the Rattar Burn on the north coast of Caithness. The workmen came across a small stone cist containing eight silver rings, a modest fortune buried in what must have seemed at the time a safe place, the local graveyard. There is no dating evidence but the most likely period for the burial of this silver is the late tenth or early eleventh century, based on the evidence of datable hoards containing ring-money (see Chapter 3).

CHAPTER FIVE

The western seaway: Argyll and the Western Isles

Much of the archaeological evidence for Viking activities in western Scotland was discovered so long ago that its value is limited, but at least, in most cases, the objects have been preserved in museums even if the details of how and where they were found are sparse. Typical is the sword-hilt found on the island of Eigg around 1830; all that is known is that it was picked up while a mound was being levelled (**60**). This may have been one of Scotland's richest Viking burials, for the sword-hilt belongs to a group of splendid swords made in Norway in the late eighth and ninth centuries. It is made of bronze with intricate decoration in silver wire and inlaid silver plates with stylized animal-motifs and gilding (NMS).

Overall, the archaeological picture in western Scotland is dominated by graves, often chance discoveries, when sand eroded from the dunes, and instantly recognizable by the human bones and distinctive grave-goods. Domestic sites can be identified in the same way, as kitchen middens, walls or paving emerge from a weathered cliff-face, but extensive excavation is needed before the nature and date of the buildings can be discovered. There are many grass-covered foundations of rectangular houses to be seen on the ground, but again without excavation these are as likely to belong to the eighteenth century as to the Viking Age.

The graves are mostly located on the islands, with a notable concentration on Colonsay, Oronsay and Islay, but it is difficult to judge how

60 *An elaborately decorated bronze and silver sword-hilt from the island of Eigg.*

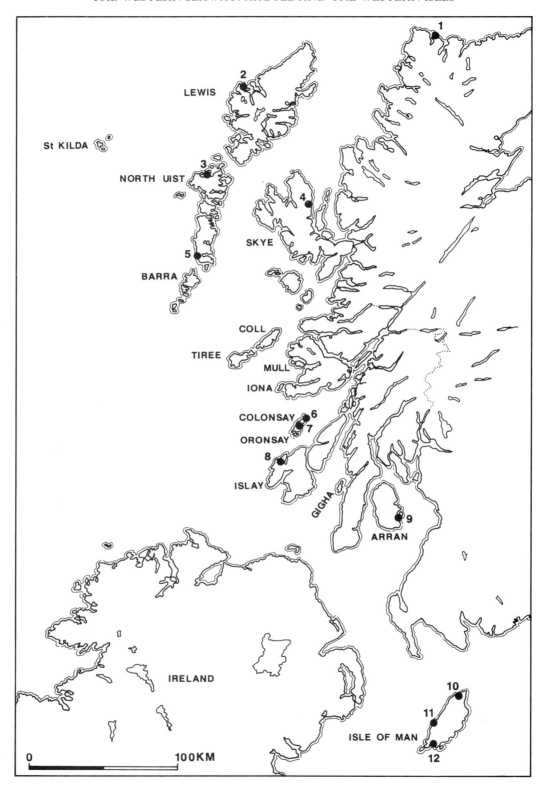

many of them indicate colonization and how many were the results of casualties of raids, buried on the way home in the first peaceful spot. Certainly, as Henry Loyn wrote, 'the magnet was undoubtedly Ireland, but the trail of iron filings left scattered down to the Irish Sea ... must not be regarded as mere accidents of fate', for they are clues both to the sea-route taken and the most likely areas for settlement.

Linguistic evidence is far more helpful in providing an overall picture of the total area that fell under Norse domination. The place-names both of the islands and of the west coast of mainland Scotland show a mixture of Norse and Gaelic elements, but the Gaelic appears to have been a later overlay on an almost entirely Scandinavian canvas rather than an early mix-ture of languages at the time of the Norse colonization. There is no means of knowing when Gaelic reappeared strongly enough to create place-names. It would certainly have happened after the Norsemen lost political power in 1266, when the Hebrides were ceded to the Scottish crown, but perhaps more likely is that the Gaelic-speaking native population grad-ually reasserted itself after the initial Norse colonization as a result of intermarriage with the newcomers. The place-names of Lewis have been more exhaustively studied than those of any other island, and there 99 out of 126 village names remain entirely Scandinavian, suggesting that the Norse colonization was very thorough.

The degree to which the newcomers domi-nated the local population may well have varied throughout the islands, however, and Lewis may not have been typical; certainly there are fewer surviving Norse names in the southern islands. Scandinavian place-names along the coast of mainland Scotland were coined mostly to identify topographical features rather than farms or settlements, particularly names of valleys incorporating the Old Norse element *dalr* (valley), perhaps suggesting that this was on the fringe of the area physically colonized by the Norsemen. The same picture is given by the archaeological evidence, for there are no known settlements and only sparse Viking finds in mainland Argyll, some of which may relate to burials but the information about their discovery is uncertain.

Graves

On the north-west coast of Colonsay lies beauti-ful Kiloran Bay with rocky cliffs on either side and a shallow sandy beach backed by grass-covered dunes, perfect for landing shallow-draught Viking boats. No trace of settlement has been found in the vicinity, but in 1882 a Viking grave was discovered in the sand-dunes, then about 183m (600ft) from the sea (62). It had already been disturbed by rabbits and perhaps people, for many of its stone slabs were visible and some were displaced, but nevertheless exca-vation that summer and again the following year revealed the burial of a man and a horse, along with a number of fine objects. The man had been laid in a crouched position on his left side in one corner of a rectangular enclosure built with upright stone slabs, and the horse was lying on its right side immediately outside the east end of the enclosure. One of the watercolour plans of the grave shows the horse surrounded by iron rivets and the enclosure full of scattered rivets, and it seems likely that the whole grave had originally been covered by an upturned boat, with the horse beneath either prow or stern. The enclosure measured 4.6 by 3.1m (15 by 10ft), and the boat must have been at least 9m (30ft) long and probably more; it is not known how much excavation took place outside the enclosure to discover the extent of the spread of rivets.

An odd aspect of the burial of the horse is that one of the bones (the metatarsal) of its hind right

61 *Map of Viking discoveries in Western Scotland and the Isle of Man mentioned in the text.*
1 *Balnakeil;* 2 *Valtos;* 3 *The Udal;* 4 *Storr Rock;*
5 *Drimore;* 6 *Kiloran Bay;* 7 *Machrins;* 8 *Ballinaby;*
9 *King's Cross Point;* 10 *Knoc y Doonee;* 11 *Peel;*
12 *Balladoole.*

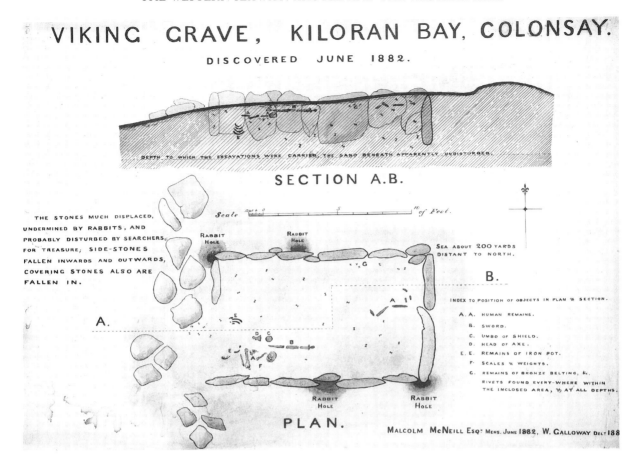

62 *Original plan of the Viking boat-burial at Kiloran Bay, Colonsay; the horse was buried outside the east end of the enclosure.*

foot had been partially severed by a massive blow which had fractured the rest of the bone, and one of the lower leg bones (the tibia) had been cut through. It seems likely that this damage had been inflicted in battle, perhaps as a result of the classic technique of cutting the hamstring to immobilize the animal. It was a fine-bred horse of about 15 hands high and perhaps 15–20 years old. Of the man we know only that he was 'of powerful build but no great stature'.

An iron strap-buckle was found beside the horse, and within the enclosure were the remains of an elaborate harness: the leather straps had rotted away leaving the decorative bronze fittings (**63**). Alongside the male burial were an iron sword and an iron axehead (**64**), both of Norwegian type, and a conical iron shield-boss. The latter appears to have been wrapped in cloth, for the clear impression of a plainly woven wool or linen cloth had been preserved on the corroded surface of the iron; the wrapping also implies that the boss had been detached from the rest of the shield. There were also a spearhead, two arrowheads, a knife, a buckle and fragments of a pot, all made of iron, a whetstone and a silver pin.

63 *(Right, above) Bronze mounts from a set of horse-harness from Kiloran Bay.*

64 *(Right, below) Iron axehead from Kiloran Bay.*

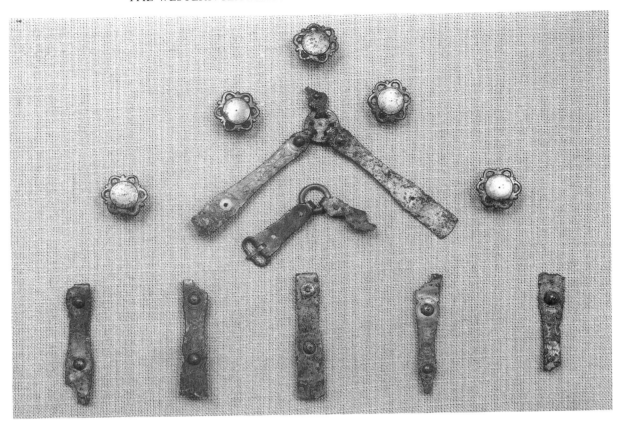

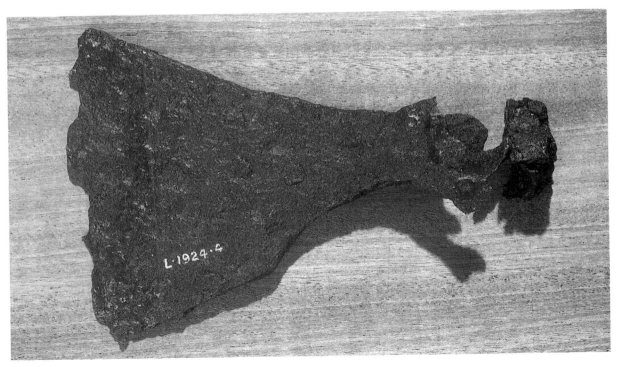

65 *Weights and scales from Kiloran Bay.*

These are all the accoutrements of a Viking warrior, but this man also carried the tools vital to trade: weights and scales for measuring silver bullion (65). Two small and shallow pans, each about 100mm (4in) across, and a bronze balance-beam survived of the scales; such pans were normally suspended from the ends of the beam by fine chains, but these were missing. The lead weights form a set of seven of various sizes, the heaviest weighing 129.6g (4½oz), and six of them are decorated with bronze or enamel mounts which have clearly been cut from larger objects. Their designs indicate that they come from fine metalwork of Scottish, Irish or Anglo-Saxon manufacture, and they are a vivid reminder of all the brooches, chalices and other items that were cut up, melted down or otherwise recycled by the Vikings.

Two Anglo-Saxon copper coins of early to mid-ninth-century date (66) were found on the site after the end of the excavation, along with a third similar coin which was lost. If these coins were part of the grave-goods, they would support a date in the latter half of the ninth century for the grave, which is also suggested by the rest of the finds (NMS).

At either end of the stone enclosure, east and west, a slab crudely incised with a Christian cross was found (67); it is not clear whether these two stones formed part of the enclosure wall or whether they were detached, and they were noticed only in the second excavation. The burial itself is of course thoroughly pagan but, if the slabs were part of the original grave-structure, the crosses imply that this Viking community had encountered and to some extent adopted Christian ideas. Whether the buried warrior had settled on Colonsay or whether he was killed in a raid on the island, we shall never know.

The fine-bred horse is more likely to have been acquired in Scotland than to have been imported from Norway. Robert Beck studied the horses carved on Pictish cross-slabs and identified two breeds. One is a small sturdy animal akin to the native ponies of Scotland, while the other is a

66 *Anglo-Saxon coin from Kiloran Bay.*

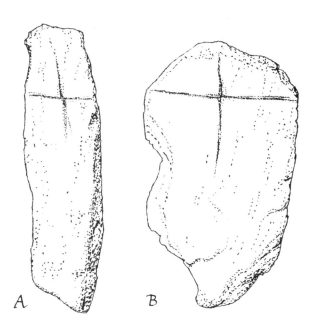

67 *Cross-incised stones from Kiloran Bay.*

larger and more elegant animal, probably deriving from Roman cavalry stock, which Robert Beck has designated the Pictish riding horse. The hunting scenes carved on Pictish stones suggest that this riding horse was thoroughly trained and carefully bred. It would be just the mount for a wealthy Viking warrior.

The Kiloran stone enclosure is unusual among Viking graves and may be related to the kerbed cairns used by the Picts in the Northern Isles and the northern mainland of Scotland. If the

Vikings were influenced by the religion of the native population, they may also have been influenced by burial customs. A similar but smaller enclosure was found in 1909 at King's Cross Point on the island of Arran; here the enclosure was covered by a cairn of stones, the burial had been cremated and the grave-goods were fragmentary, but they included part of a whalebone plaque (see p.46) and an Anglo-Saxon coin of the mid ninth century (NMS).

One other boat burial has been found in the Hebrides, on Oronsay, the close neighbour to Colonsay. It was in a low natural mound among sand-dunes on the east side of the island, partially excavated in two days in 1891 and unfortunately very poorly recorded. Two burials, thought to be those of an elderly man and woman, were found lying fully extended and accompanied by a few grave-goods of no great status, and beside them was a thick layer of charcoal containing a large number of boat-rivets and a steatite line-sinker or fisherman's weight. This is a particularly tantalizing discovery because it is impossible to draw any conclusions about the size of the boat, whether it was truly burnt (which seems odd in connection with inhumation burials) or simply rotted, and whether it was really part of the same burial as the two old people. The story is further complicated by a third grave uncovered 22 years later on the perimeter of the mound: a woman buried with a pair of oval brooches, a ring-pin, a bone needle-case and iron shears (NMS). The brooches are amongst the earliest Scandinavian finds from Scotland and confirm that raiding was quickly followed by settlement. As the mound was poorly and not even fully excavated, we have only a very limited understanding of what went on here.

The weights and scales found at Kiloran Bay can be matched not too far away by a discovery made on the small island of Gigha in 1849. In the sand-dunes at East Tarbert Bay was found a small square cist or box of stone slabs, covered by a large boulder and containing bronze scales and weights of Viking type (Hunterian Museum,

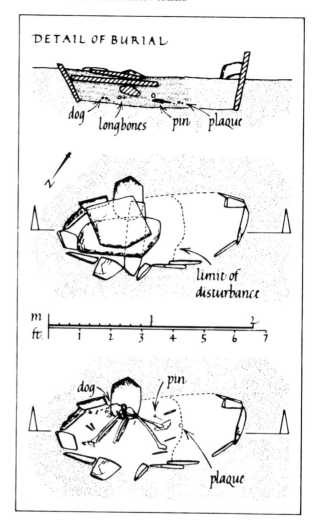

68 *Plan of a female grave at Machrins.*

Glasgow). This is often assumed to have been a burial, but it is more likely to have been a safe-keeping place – there are other cases where something of value was hidden in a small cist, such as the ecclesiastical bell at Saevar Howe in Orkney, or in a wooden container such as the silver hoard from Burray in Orkney. The scale-pans from Gigha are made of bronze plated with tin, so that the incised geometric decoration cuts through the silvery tin to show the contrasting golden bronze below. The balance-beam folds up, ideal for travelling, and there are small

69 *The sandy grasslands at Machrins, Colonsay, were a focus for early historic settlement.*

bronze birds to decorate each end of the beam, although only one arm of the beam survives. The four lead weights are undecorated.

These two discoveries of weighing scales and lead weights are often interpreted as both underlining the use of the western seaways for trade and emphasizing an apparent difference between the Viking settlement of western Scotland and that of northern Scotland, where no such finds have been made. This highlights a real problem in Viking studies in Scotland (and elsewhere in the Atlantic colonies): the samples are too small to be the basis from which to argue broad patterns of behaviour. The ability to weigh out silver bullion was as essential to the Viking warlord, wanting to keep his men happy, as it was to the merchant – and the concept of the lone merchant plying his trade may be quite inappropriate to the Vikings in the west.

Two other graves on Colonsay have yielded evidence of animals, both located in the sand-dunes at Machrins. A mound explored in 1891 contained a male burial with an iron axe, sword, spearhead and shield-boss, a single amber bead, a bronze dress-pin and penannular brooch, and horse harness (NMS), along with bones of a horse. Almost a century later, a female burial in an oval cist was excavated; one end of the cist had been disturbed by rabbits and only the lower part of the skeleton of a middle-aged woman survived, lying on her right side with her legs flexed (**68**). The body of a small dog had been laid beside her with its head on her knees. The dog was about six years old, heavily built with short bow-legs and very similar to a modern Welsh corgi. There was no evidence of how it had died, but it is likely to have had its throat cut. The link between lap-dogs and women is so marked in early Irish literature that it has been argued that the dogs were used as comforters to soothe period pains, the equivalent of modern hot-water bottles.

This is one of the few burials to have been dated by radiocarbon analysis of the bones, yielding a date centred around AD 800; none of the grave-goods is Scandinavian in origin, but it is clearly a pagan burial and at this period the local Scots of Dalriada ought to have been thoroughly Christian. A bronze ring-pin was found at the thigh of the woman and had probably fastened the shroud (70); a fragment of

70 *Bronze ring-pin from a grave at Machrins.*

71 *Grave-goods from a female burial at Valtos, Lewis.*

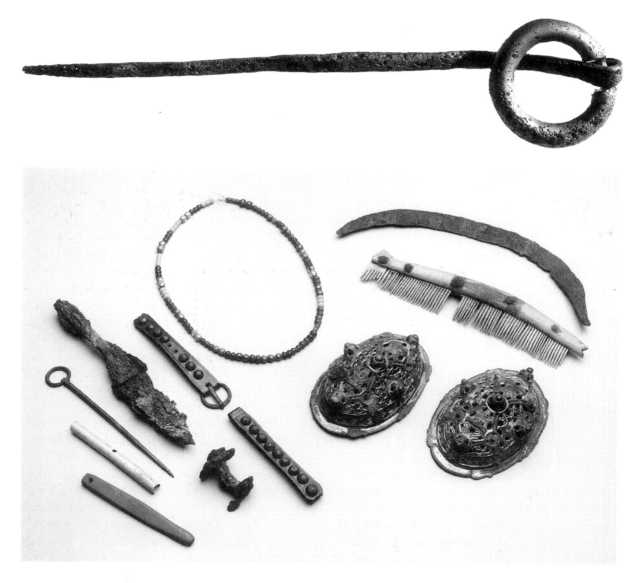

72 Iron sword, shield-boss and hand-grip from a male grave at Ballinaby, Islay.

textile suggests that the latter was made of finely woven linen. There were also the remains of an iron knife and a fragment of decorated bronze, the latter apparently reused from some larger object. The grave was only 14m (46ft) from a native settlement of broadly contemporary date, but there is no means of establishing whether the two were connected in any way.

These Colonsay graves are all isolated single burials, but there were small cemeteries elsewhere in the Western Isles, indicating areas where settlement was either long-lived or more dense. One such area was Valtos on the northwest coast of Lewis, where the sea has created small islands, sea-lochs and sandy beaches, forming one of the most glorious vistas of the Western Isles. Three Viking burials have been found here, in 1979, 1991 and 1992, including a woman and a child of about six years. It seems likely that they were part of a larger cemetery and that this landscape of sandy grasslands was once a focus for Viking settlement.

The grave found in 1979 was that of a woman of substance, despite the fact that she had apparently been buried simply in a pit rather than in any more elaborate structure; aged between 35 and 40 years, she was lying on her back, dressed in a fine linen tunic and pinafore, with two oval brooches at her shoulders, a string of 44 brightly coloured glass beads which may have hung between the two brooches, a bronze ring-pin, a matching set of bronze belt-buckle and strap-end, a bone comb, an iron knife, a whetstone, a bone needle-case containing the remains of two iron needles and an iron sickle (71). The two oval brooches look very similar but are not in fact a matching pair, though they could probably have been sold as such. They and the ring-pin suggest that this burial took place in the tenth century. Another wealthy female grave had been found in the area in 1915, wearing not only Scandinavian brooches but also two brooches and a belt-buckle of native design.

Intriguing among early records of grave discoveries is the reference to a number of male burials and horse bones found in the eighteenth century at Cornaigbeg on Tiree; this sounds like a rich cemetery, for some of the swords had hilts decorated with silver, but all the finds are lost. Similarly at Ballinaby on Islay, where at least three pagan burials have been recorded in 1877 and 1932, there is an eighteenth-century record of many other human bones and weapons (now lost) which may indicate that there was once a cemetery of some size here. The three known burials were accompanied by a range of high-status grave-goods: two males had swords (72), axes, shield-bosses, a spear, hammer and tongs (73), part of an iron cauldron and the bronze terminal from a drinking horn, while the female grave contained a pair of oval brooches (74), three bronze ornaments, a fine silver dress-pin

73 *Iron axes, hammer and tongs from Ballinaby.*

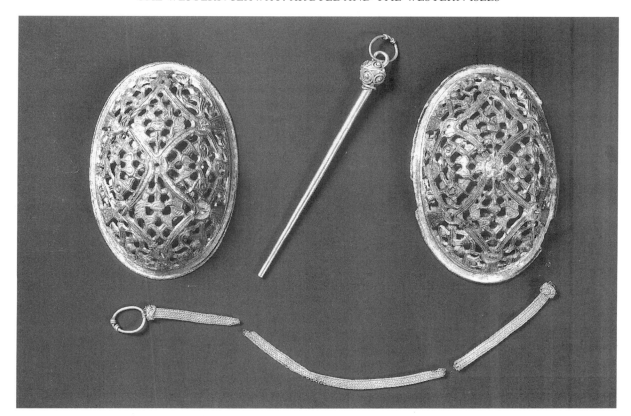

74 *Oval brooches, silver pin and safety-chain from a female grave at Ballinaby.*

with filigree decoration and safety-chain, twelve beads (including amber and jet; 75), a bronze ladle (76), sewing equipment, a glass linen smoother (see 75) and an iron heckle for the preparation of flax fibres. A little distance away, a pair of fine oval brooches was found beside a great standing stone, probably marking another Viking burial. Ballinaby is close to the west coast of Islay, where there are good sandy bays for landing boats and fertile land for farming, as well as access to the Irish Sea.

Viking graves on the Isle of Man

There are clear links between some of the graves in the southern Hebrides and the Isle of Man: the horse harness from Kiloran Bay, for example, is very similar to harness found in the contemporary Manx boat-burials at Balladoole and Knoc y Doonee. The Isle of Man must have been an invaluable springboard for raids on Ireland from

75 *Glass linen smoother and beads from Ballinaby.*

76 Bronze ladle from Ballinaby.

the onset of Viking activities, and in the tenth century the Irish Sea became, in the words of Barbara Crawford, 'a Celto-Norse lake', dominated by the Norsemen. There are very few early female Scandinavian graves on Man and the impression of the island in the tenth century is one of warrior overlords marrying local girls. Excavations in the 1980s on the site of Peel Castle uncovered an early Christian chapel and cemetery to which pagan Norse graves were added in the mid tenth century, including the burial of a woman with a fine range of grave-goods. These included an iron cooking spit, knives, shears, a bone comb, needles in a case and a splendid necklace of 71 beads, mostly of glass. Two other burials contained small silver balls, which appear to have adorned the fringes of cloaks or tunics.

These pagan graves belong to a time when Christianity was gaining a hold on the Norse community, and the fact that the Peel burials used the same grave-structure, the long cist (in Man known as the lintel grave), and the same east–west orientation as the Christian graves in the cemetery reinforces the impression of a community whose religious allegiances were in a state of flux. Tenth-century Manx cross-slabs show a similar mixture of pagan and Christian motifs, and their runic inscriptions include both Scandinavian and native Celtic personal names –

and the strength of Norse settlement is demonstrated by the sheer number of runestones (29), almost as many as in Norway (33).

Sculpture

The close links between Man and the southern Scottish islands continued through the tenth century: it has even been argued that the famous Manx sculptor, Gautr Bjornson, was a native of the island of Coll. Although Scotland lacks the quantity of Viking sculpture that survives in Man, there is a cross-slab from Kilbar on the island of Barra on which the decoration is clearly related to the work of the Manx sculptors. There are such close similarities in art style between the Manx cross-slabs and the silver hoard found at Skaill in Orkney (see pp.72–5) that the craftsman who made the Skaill brooches may have been trained on the Isle of Man.

Two later pieces of sculpture in Scandinavian taste are worth mentioning. From Doid Mhairi near Port Ellen in Islay (now in NMS) there is an eleventh-century cross-slab decorated with distinctive foliage ornament in the style known as Ringerike (named after the sandstone around Oslo in Norway from which slabs were cut and

77 *Cross-slab with runic inscription from Iona.*

decorated in this style), while Iona has a cross-slab of slightly later date with a runic inscription (77). The slab and the inscription are damaged, but the surviving portion reads 'Kali son of Aulus laid this stone over (his) brother Fugl' (see Chapter 7 for runes). The museum on Iona also has the lower part of a splendid cross-slab carved with a boat and a smith with his tools. The monastery was attacked several times in the late eighth and ninth centuries, and excavation has uncovered evidence of burning which may be the result of one of these attacks but may equally well relate to some domestic accident. Several gravestones and cross-slabs show Scandinavian patronage in the tenth and eleventh centuries – after their conversion to Christianity, the Norsemen shared Scottish and Irish veneration for Iona. There were however still troubled moments to come, during one of which a large hoard of silver was buried close to the Abbey; this was discovered in 1950 and consists of about 350 coins, mostly Anglo-Saxon, a silver ingot, a silver and gold decorative mounting and a small loop of gold wire (NMS).

Settlements

The single most important excavation of a settlement in western Scotland is the Udal on North Uist, where a long sequence includes both pre-Norse and Norse activity, but in the absence of the long-awaited publication of the results of this work only a bare outline can be offered here. The pre-Norse settlement (above p.21) was abruptly replaced, probably in the middle of the ninth century, by Norse buildings and artefacts, including a small sub-rectangular fort with massive stone walls. This is the only early Norse fortification known in Scotland and it implies that, in the Outer Hebrides at least, there was initial and perhaps even successful opposition from the ousted native population. The life of the fort was judged by the excavator to have been very short, probably only the first decade or so of the Norse occupation. Elsewhere the Vikings may have taken over existing fortified

78 *Plan of the early Norse house at Drimore, South Uist.*

tected nearby (**78**). In places there were inner and outer faces to the house wall, but mostly there was a single facing of stones set against the sand, and only the basal courses of the wall survived. The core of the wall is likely to have been turf. The internal floor-area measured about 14 by 5m (46 by 16ft), a substantial size for such a flimsily built structure – was this perhaps a temporary shelter? The floor deposits were minimal, again suggesting a short occupation, although there were bones of domestic cattle, sheep, pig, dog and horse. Artefacts left on the floor included a fine example of a hogback bone comb with interlaced decoration (**79**), a conical bone playing-piece (with a socket in its base to take a peg), and two unusual items: a whalebone cleaver probably used in the preparation of leather (**80**), and a bone door-sneck or latch (**81**). The cleaver is a Scandinavian type of tool and in Norway is dated to the later ninth century, a date suitable also for the comb.

These two settlements suggest that colonization of the Western Isles was underway in the second half of the ninth century, somewhat later than in the Northern Isles, but two is a very small sample on which to base conclusions. There is great need for more Norse sites to be identified and excavated in this area. Skye is an obvious candidate for investigation: place-names indicate extensive Scandinavian settlement in the north and west of the island, and the discovery of three gold finger-rings and three hoards of silver implies that there was considerable wealth among the Norse families of the tenth century. Intensive fieldwork by the Royal Commission on the Ancient and Historical Monuments of Scotland in the Waternish peninsula in northern Skye revealed rectilinear house-foundations most of which are likely to be post-medieval but some of which may overlie earlier settlements.

In a few cases, the location of a Viking settlement has been identified through chance finds but nothing is known about the form or extent of the site. For example, there is a Viking domestic midden eroding on the west coast of Lewis which has yielded two ring-pins, an

sites. Coastal forts and duns containing rectangular house-foundations would reward examination, for without excavation the date of such secondary structures could be Norse, medieval or later.

The only other excavated early Norse settlement in the Western Isles was at Drimore on the west coast of South Uist, where a few stones protruding from the sand led to the discovery of a single, rather irregularly built house; it was covered by up to 1.5m (5ft) of windblown sand, and, as only the immediate area of the building was excavated, others could have lain unde-

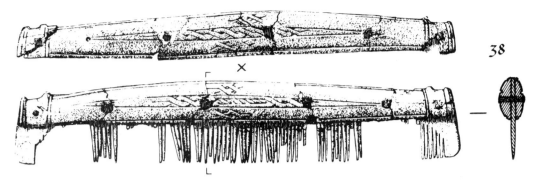

79 (Above) Viking bone comb from Drimore.

80 (Right) Whalebone cleaver from Drimore.

Anglo-Saxon coin and an enamelled mount similar to those decorating the weights in the Kiloran grave, but little trace of associated buildings has been recorded. Viking settlement is often claimed on the remote islands of St Kilda, 64km (40 miles) west of the Outer Hebrides, based on their Norse name (St Kilda is probably derived from Old Norse *skildir*, shields, while Hirta comes from *hirtir*, stags) and the discovery of a pair of oval brooches. Nothing is known about how or exactly where the brooches were found, but they are likely to have come from a female Norse grave. Neither names nor brooches prove that the islands were settled by the Norsemen, however, and it is equally possible that the woman died during some ill-fated voyage, her vessel blown off course by bad weather.

Excavated settlements in western Scotland are thus so few that it is impossible to be specific about their overall economy, but it is likely that they maintained a life-style similar to that in the Northern Isles. This was based on a combination of mixed farming and fishing, supplemented by the proceeds of raiding which could be used both to augment family wealth and also to buy other goods.

Some of that wealth was buried for safety and never recovered: silver hoards of Scandinavian type have been found in Lewis, North Uist, Skye, Tiree, Mull, Iona, Islay and on mainland Argyll at Kilmartin. Most of these belong to the late tenth or early eleventh centuries, but one of the Skye hoards is the earliest known from Scotland, dated by its coins to around 935. This particular example was discovered on the beach below the Storr Rock near Portree, and it consisted of 110 coins and 23 pieces of hack-silver, including Arabic coins together with part of a spiral-ring from the Baltic.

81 *Bone door-sneck from Drimore.*

None of the graves or settlements in western Scotland described here is visible on the ground today, but it is worth visiting the places where they were found in order to gain a visual impression of the areas favoured for settlement by the early Norse colonists – their taste for beauty spots was impeccable.

CHAPTER SIX

The Viking fringe: southern and eastern Scotland

Surprisingly, the far south-west of Scotland, the area known as Galloway, seems not to have been settled to any marked extent by Scandinavians, despite its proximity to the Norse Isle of Man and the Danish settlement of Cumbria. The Rhins of Galloway were after all one side of the marine corridor into the Irish Sea. Modern work examining archaeological, historical and linguistic evidence all points to the same conclusion, that the Scandinavian element was very limited.

Scandinavian elements in the place-names of southern and eastern Scotland are more difficult to interpret than those in northern and western areas. Some contain Norse personal names allied to English or Gaelic elements, such as Dolphington, derived from the Old Norse name *Dolgfinnr* and the Old English word *tun* meaning enclosure; these are not early place-names and are unlikely to represent Scandinavian speakers (Dolgfinnr may not even have been of Scandinavian descent). More certain ground is reached with names containing the Old Danish element *-by* or *-bie*, meaning farmstead or village, such as Sorbie, for these are likely to indicate genuine settlement of people who had moved northwards from the widespread Scandinavian population of northern England (82). This is particularly clear in the area around the head of the Solway Firth, where settlement spread northwards from Cumbria and left a dense scatter of names ending in -by or -bie, all of which were probably coined before the middle of the tenth century. A very few such names are to be found to the west around Kirkcudbright and Whithorn, and these are considered to represent settlement by sea from the coast of Scandinavian Cumbria. Farther north a few such names south of the Forth and Clyde estuaries, in Fife and immediately north of the Tay estuary, may represent a very minor Scandinavian component in the population, which could be either Danish or Norwegian in origin (Old Norse *byr* has the same meaning and gives rise to similar place-names as the Old Danish *by*).

Apart from the concentrated settlement around the head of the Solway Firth, place-name evidence thus indicates only rare Scandinavian settlement in southern and eastern Scotland, and it seems likely that the people involved were there in order to trade with the Scots and English. *Orkneyinga Saga* mentions a merchant named Knut who spent a lot of time at Berwick in the twelfth century (chapter 93), and the three great estuaries of the Clyde, Forth and Tay would have attracted traders as well as raiding Vikings from an early period. Some were wealthy enough to commission a special type of gravestone, known to us as the hogback, which was invented in the tenth century among Scandinavian communities in Yorkshire and Cumbria. The distribution of hogbacks in southern and eastern Scotland is very similar to that found for Scandinavian place-names, with a noticeable preference for coastal and river-valley locations.

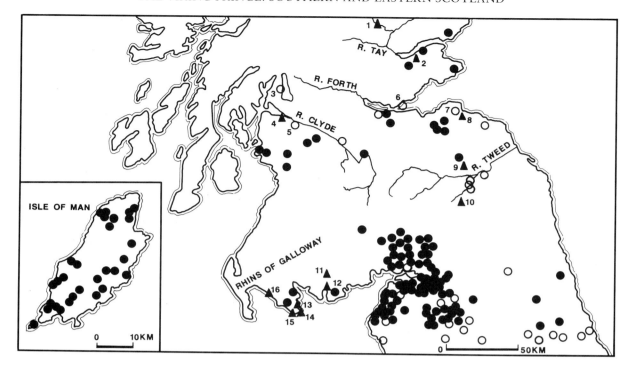

Hogback monuments

The typical hogback tombstone is a solid block of stone carved into the shape of a house with a convex curve (hence 'hogback') to the ridge of its gabled roof (83). The tiles of the roof are usually sculpted, and the most elaborate and attractive examples have animals carved at their gables. The hogback has no ancestry in Scandinavia and seems to have developed in northern England as a unique response to local tastes, influenced by contemporary architecture, by existing Christian traditions of house-shaped shrines to hold the relics of saints and by a love of animal ornament that was common both to the Scandinavians and to the peoples of the British Isles.

It is often assumed that, because some early hogbacks are decorated with scenes from pagan Scandinavian mythology, they must have evolved in a pagan secular context, later to become Christian. Although this is certainly possible, there are good precedents for the inclusion of pagan motifs on overtly Christian artefacts such as cross-slabs, and the idea of a

82 *Map of southern Scotland showing the distribution of Scandinavian -byr place-names (solid dots), hogbacks (open dots), and Viking discoveries mentioned in the text. 1 Dunkeld; 2 Lindores; 3 Luss; 4 Port Glasgow; 5 Govan; 6 Inchcolm; 7 Tyninghame; 8 Dunbar; 9 Gordon; 10 Jedburgh; 11 Talnotrie; 12 Kirkcudbright; 13 Whithorn; 14 Isle of Whithorn; 15 St Ninian's Cave; 16 Chapel Finian.*

recumbent stone monument covering the grave is itself Christian in origin. It is unlikely, moreover, that the expertise required for monumental stone-carving could be found other than in an ecclesiastical context. In Scotland, the earliest hogbacks are to be found at existing centres of Christianity: Govan (see 83) on the Clyde, Meigle (see 84) in Perthshire, Brechin in Angus and, probably, the island of Inchcolm in the Firth of Forth (colour plate 8).

As a rare three-dimensional form of sculpture, the hogback gave the stone-carver an oppor-

83 *The early hogback tombstone in Govan Old Parish Church, Glasgow.*

tunity to explore more fully the possibilities of his craft. In some cases great beasts are carved clasping either end of the stone, as at Inchcolm, and in others animals straddle the stone, as at Govan, or gaze out from one end, as at Brechin and Meigle. English influence is clearly to be seen on the early hogbacks at Govan, Inchcolm and Tyninghame, but once established in Scotland the hogback tradition developed according to local tastes and appears to have remained popular in eastern Scotland and the far north for longer than in England. For some reason in western Scotland the fashion spread no farther north and west than Luss on the shore of Loch Lomond. None has been found in the Hebrides or in the Isle of Man, and only one in Ireland.

Govan boasts five hogbacks dating from the tenth century, mostly of considerable size; the earliest is the smallest, a slim and highly arched hogback (83), close in style to English examples of the mid-tenth century in Cumbria. The other four are remarkable for their massive size, unrivalled elsewhere in Scotland or England. They were all found in the churchyard but there is no record of any associated burials and they may well have been moved. Very little is known about the original contexts of hogbacks either in Scotland or England, and their interpretation as tombstones is an assumption, though a very reasonable one. The example on the island of

97

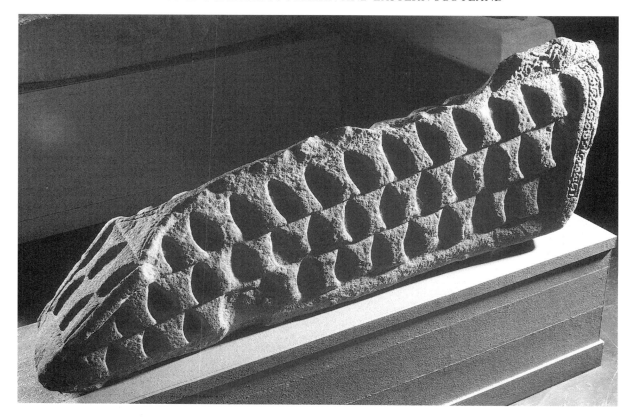

84 *Hogback tombstone amongst the collection of early Christian sculpture in the museum at Meigle.*

Inchcolm in the Firth of Forth may well be in its original position, and according to a sixteenth-century record there was a standing cross beside it, reinforcing the idea that it marked a grave. If the Govan hogbacks had originally been accompanied by crosses, the group would have had a stunning impact as a monumental grave-group. There was already in eastern Scotland a tradition of recumbent grave-covers with a slot at one end to take an upright cross. Elaborately decorated examples can be seen in the museums at Meigle and St Vigeans, and the Meigle hogback (**84**), created in the late tenth century, is closely related in art style to the earlier products of the Meigle stonemasons' workshop. It is also an idiosyncratic shape compared to most hogbacks, being wedge-shaped rather than hogbacked.

Another idiosyncratic stone exists at Brechin, like Meigle in the heart of the area that was formerly southern Pictland with its strong traditions of stonecarving. In what was now

politically the land of the Scots, those traditions continued to flourish but with Irish overtones which can be detected in the style of both the foliage and the great animal head on the Brechin hogback, which was carved in the early eleventh century. It is an unusually low monument, which enabled it to be turned over and reused as a grave-cover probably in the seventeenth century.

Despite the links between Govan on the Firth of Clyde and Cumbria, there are only two hogbacks between those two areas, at Dalserf on the upper Clyde and from Mossknow in Dumfriesshire (now in Dumfries Museum). To the east, the distribution of eleventh-century hogbacks stretches from Berwickshire via Fife to Orkney and Shetland (Chapter 7), and is one facet of the tangible seaborne links between the

Church in eastern Scotland and the far north that began in Pictish times in the eighth century and peaked with the building of St Magnus Cathedral in Kirkwall in the twelfth.

85 *Aerial view of Whithorn Priory and excavations by the Whithorn Trust (in the field between the churchyard and the main street).*

Whithorn

Whithorn was a most important ecclesiastical centre from the late fifth century onwards and the focus of the cult of St Ninian for more than a thousand years, but its location is difficult to explain. Transport by sea was essential both for pilgrims and trade, but Whithorn lies some 5km (3 miles) from the natural harbour at the Isle of Whithorn on the south coast. It is thought that Ninian was sent to an existing enclave of Christians, and the foundation of his bishopric

and monastery at Whithorn must relate to the location of that community. The British monastery had been taken over by the Anglian Northumbrians by 731 when the English historian Bede refers to the Northumbrian bishopric based there. Whithorn flourished under Northumbrian rule until the 830s, when it appears to have entered a period of decline, in the course of which the church was abandoned and destroyed by fire. There is no evidence to suggest that the monastery suffered a devastating Viking attack, and its abandonment is more likely to relate to the political situation in the heart of Northumbria, for York fell to the Vikings in 867.

Our understanding of the detailed sequence at Whithorn comes from excavations by the archaeologists working for Peter Hill and the Whithorn Trust since 1985, and the story is becoming clearer every year. Traces of buildings on either side of an ancient track belong to a phase of settlement lasting from around 850 until about 1000, and the finds include late Northumbrian coins, a Scandinavian harness-fitting, antler combs and ring-pins. This evidence suggests that the community had contact with the Scandinavians but not that it was a Viking settlement at this period. There are about twenty-five cross-slabs of tenth-century date from the site, testifying to its continuing importance as an ecclesiastical centre. Some twenty more such slabs are known from the countryside around Whithorn.

The subsequent phase of occupation from around 1000 to the mid-twelfth century has a greater Scandinavian flavour, and it has been argued that Whithorn was now an Hiberno-Norse trading-post. The Hibernian or Irish connection lies in the timber houses, several of which were well-preserved owing to damp soil conditions; these were square houses with rounded corners and central hearths, and they are best paralleled in Viking Dublin and Waterford in Ireland. The use of this type of house may even suggest that their occupants came from the Irish Viking towns. There were numerous phases of rebuilding as the original houses decayed, indicating a thriving community. Amongst the finds are Scandinavian artefacts such as bronze pins of a type known to the archaeologist as stick-pins, glass beads, soapstone artefacts and whetstones. There is also the wooden beam from a set of weighing-scales and a lead weight decorated with a bronze mount, underlining the trading aspect of the settlement. Local resources were used to manufacture various goods of leather, antler and metal, which could be exchanged for imported items.

No trace has been found yet of a church

86 *Cross-slab in the museum at Whithorn.*

belonging to this Viking phase at Whithorn, but the excavated area is only a fraction of the whole. After a period in which documentary sources are lacking, we know that the bishopric was revived in about 1128 and that a new church was built, part of which was incorporated into the thirteenth-century priory church, the walls of which may still be seen (88). The graves of thirteenth- and fourteenth-century bishops and priors were uncovered by previous excavations, accompanied by gold rings, silver communion vessels and a splendidly ornate crozier. Recent work has shown that the layout of the Viking trading-post survived into the mid-thirteenth century but that a new type of building was adopted from the mid-twelfth century. The manufacture of goods continued, but trade contacts appear to have been with eastern Scotland and England rather than across the Irish Sea.

A fine natural harbour exists at the Isle of Whithorn, between the island and the mainland on the west side (89). The island is now linked to the mainland by a causeway, but there can never have been a problem over access to the island even without the causeway, because at low tide the inlet is virtually dry. There are the ruins of a church, known as St Ninian's Chapel, on the island, which is thought to have been built around 1300 to service the many pilgrims arriving by sea to visit Whithorn. It is likely to have replaced an earlier chapel, for the pilgrimage tradition began centuries before and excavations have uncovered traces of a previous chancel. The foundations of another chapel, thought to have been built in the tenth or eleventh century for the use of pilgrims from Ireland, may be seen on the west coast of the Machars near Mochrum, some 19km (12 miles) north-west of Whithorn. Known as Chapel Finian, this was a small rectangular building set within an enclosure, very similar in layout to the contemporary chapel on the Brough of Deerness in Orkney (Chapter 7). St Finian was a sixth-century Irish monk.

Following the example of St Martin of Tours in France, caves were often used as refuges from the bustle of monastic life by monks wishing peace for meditation. St Ninian is associated with such a cave on the south coast of the Machars at Glasserton, about 5km (3 miles)

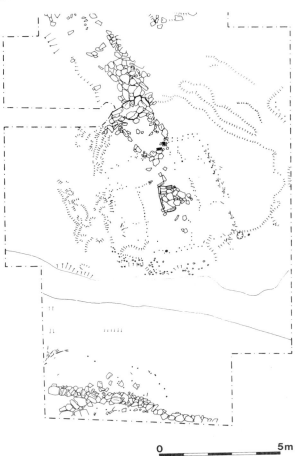

87 *Plan of an eleventh-century Norse house at Whithorn; a stone hearth is central within a square house built of wooden stakes and wattling, and the doorway is paved.*

from Whithorn, and the cave continued to be used, by pilgrims if not by monks for meditation, into medieval times. Crosses of types datable to the eighth and ninth centuries are carved on the rock face on the west side of the cave, and free-standing cross-slabs and cross-incised boulders found in the cave may be seen in the museum at Whithorn (90).

Viking lost property

Although southern and eastern Scotland were not intensively settled by Scandinavians, as were

101

the north and west, few areas can have escaped the effects of Viking activities, and in eastern Scotland there were sporadic threats from Danish as well as Norwegian Vikings. Such activity, either raiding or trading, accounts for the isolated finds of Viking artefacts and silver hoards, such as the gold finger-ring from Annandale in Dumfriesshire and the oval brooches from Perthshire. Recent excavations at Dunbar on the coast of East Lothian yielded both a Scandinavian comb and coins indicating trading links with Viking York. It can be difficult to distinguish between Viking hoards and native hoards which contain Viking material, although both are likely to relate to the troubled times created by the presence of the Vikings. A hoard from Talnotrie in Kirkcudbrightshire, buried around 875, contains a gold finger-ring, a decorated lead weight and Anglo-Saxon ornaments, along with spindle-whorls and wax and imported silver coins. This is considered to have been a native hoard, although the coins may well have been acquired through trade with the Scandinavians.

A hoard found at Gordon in Berwickshire (now lost) appears to have been purely Viking in character, for it consisted of a Scandinavian type of gold finger-ring, part of a Hiberno-Norse arm-ring, part of an Irish pin and two silver ingots, all of which suggest that the hoard was buried sometime in the first half of the tenth century. Its presence in inland Berwickshire may have been connected with known Viking raids on southern Scotland, just as the Viking hoard of silver coins and arm-rings discovered near Port Glasgow on the river Clyde may have been a result of a plundering trip down the west of Scotland by Vikings from Orkney in the 980s, which is recorded in *Njal's Saga*.

88 *(Left, above) The twelfth-century Priory Church at Whithorn.*

89 *(Left, below) The Isle of Whithorn is now linked to the mainland; St Ninian's Chapel was built on the island around* AD *1300.*

90 *Cross-slab from St Ninian's Cave, now in the museum at Whithorn.*

Two silver hoards dating from around 1025 were found in south-east Scotland at Jedburgh in Roxburghshire and Lindores in Fife; both contain coins of King Cnut of England and they may be related to the struggle between Scotland and England for political control of Northumbria in the early eleventh century.

Apart from the Lindores hoard and the isolated finds of Scandinavian objects from Perthshire, the fertile heartlands of Scotland between the Firth of Forth and the Dornoch Firth are remarkably free of material traces of Viking activities. Raids took place certainly: the monastic annals tell of a slaughter 'beyond counting' of the men of Fortriu by the 'gentiles' or Vikings in 839. Fortriu was a former sub-kingdom of the Picts, centred on Strathearn in central Scotland between the upper waters of the Forth and Tay. These two great rivers led the Vikings into the heart of Scotland. The rich monastery at Dunkeld on the Tay was particularly vulnerable, and it was targeted for attack by Ivar II from Viking Dublin in 903. Around 975, a hoard of silver coins and ring-money was buried near the monastery at Tarbat on the coast of Easter Ross; this is likely to relate to the activities either of Norsemen from the Northern Isles or Danes from England.

The great Pictish fort at Burghead on the south coast of the Moray Firth suffered a devastating attack sometime in the late ninth or early tenth century. This is known from archaeological evidence dated by radiocarbon analysis, but it is impossible to be certain whether the attackers were Vikings or Scots. The Scots of Dalriada had finally taken political control of Pictland in the mid-ninth century, and Moray may well have attempted to hold out against them. Burghead is likely to have had long-established trading links with the Northern Isles, making it an obvious target for Viking attack as well. A great battle is the subject of the carved panels on the back of Sueno's Stone at Forres (**91**), some 12km (7 miles) from Burghead. This superb cross-slab, more than 6.5m (21ft) high and intricately carved in relief, is thought to date from the ninth or tenth centuries, to judge by the style of the sculpture. Does it commemorate an epic struggle during which Burghead was burned and many of the men of Moray lost their lives?

91 *Sueno's Stone, Forres, before it was protected by a glass enclosure.*

CHAPTER SEVEN

After the Vikings: late Norse Scotland AD 1100–1300

The most popular image of Scandinavian Scotland, which appears on anything from tea-towels to gas-fires, is an ivory chessman (**92**). A rook in the game, this is a helmeted footsoldier portrayed as a berserk with glaring eyes and huge bared teeth sunk into the top of his shield, very much the image of the bloodthirsty Viking. He is one of a great hoard of chessmen (**93**) found in a stone cist in a sand-dune at Uig Bay on the west coast of the island of Lewis in 1831; there were at least 93 items, consisting of 78 chessmen, 14 plain draughtsmen and a belt buckle, all carved from walrus ivory. The British Museum paid £84 for 67 chessmen, the draughtsmen and the buckle in the November of 1831, and another 11 chessmen were acquired by the National Museum of Antiquities of Scotland 57 years later, implying that there may originally have been even more in the hoard. The chessmen are beautifully carved, unique for their high quality as well as for their quantity: with 8 kings, 8 queens, 16 bishops, 15 knights, 12 rooks and 19 pawns, the hoard represents four chess sets (missing are 1 knight, 4 rooks and 45 pawns). When they were first found, traces of colour showed that originally some of the pieces had been stained dark red, so as to distinguish between the chessmen of each player, but no colour survives today.

92 *Ivory chessman from Lewis; this powerful image of a marauding Viking was a rook in the game.*

93 *Some of the Lewis chessmen, a superb set of twelfth-century pieces.*

The chessmen can be dated by the art style of the panels of decoration on the chair-backs of the kings, queens and some of the bishops. These contain vigorous designs of animals and foliage which are comparable to the carving on Norwegian stave-built churches and on the doorways of Ely Cathedral in eastern England, as well as to a number of other ivories, indicating a date around the middle of the twelfth century. Where the chessmen were made is impossible to determine, but it was certainly within a Scandinavian cultural framework, and Norway is probably the strongest candidate. How they came to be hidden on Lewis will never be known – perhaps some merchant was forced to bury his valuable stock for safety and failed to return. A very similar chess piece was found during excavations in the twelfth-century church of St Olaf in Trondheim in northern Norway; unfortunately, the excavations took place in the late nineteenth century and only a drawing survives of the piece. It was the upper part of a queen, and she had the same staring eyes and strong facial features as the Lewis pieces.

The Lewis rook may be a vivid image of a marauding Viking, but the kings, queens and bishops convey a more accurate image of twelfth-century life. The Viking heyday was long over, the adventurers were replaced by landowners and the cultural achievements of the earldom were on a par with the rest of Europe, with all the proper machinery of State and Church. Beyond Scandinavian Scotland, the Viking world had shrunk in the middle years of the eleventh century; political control had been lost in Russia to the east and in Ireland to the west, and William of Normandy, himself descended from Viking forebears, had conquered England. In Scotland, the Western Isles continued to be ruled for Norway but the local lordship changed hands. They were ruled by the king of the Isle of Man until the mid-twelfth century, when in two battles in 1156 and 1158 Somerled, Lord of Argyll, defeated the Manx

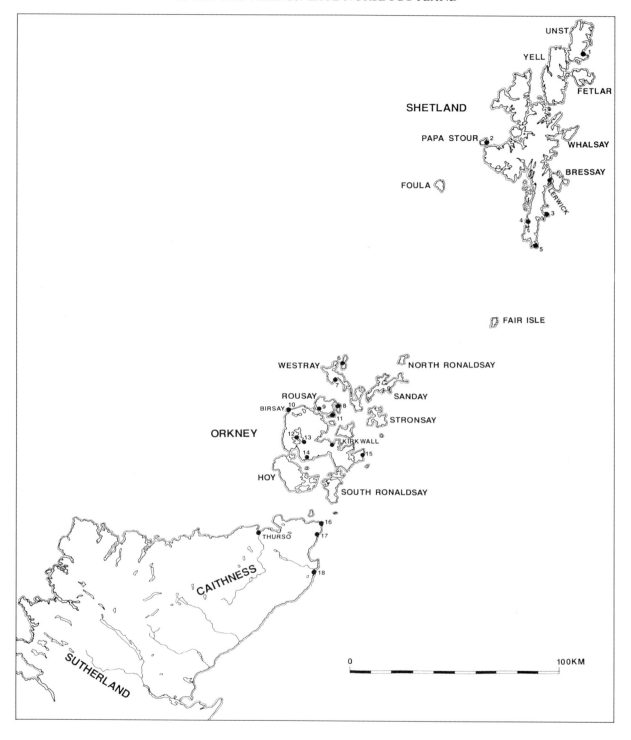

king and added most of the Isles to his lordship. Skye and Lewis remained under the control of Man. The whole of the mainland north of Moray was in theory part of the kingdom of the Scots, but in reality it was dominated by the Norse earldom of Orkney and Caithness.

The sagas, especially *Orkneyinga Saga*, convey a vivid impression of twelfth-century life among the leading Norse families in the earl-dom, centred on Orkney and Caithness: power struggles, killings, feasts, voyages and pilgri-mages. There are hints of the duties of running family estates, of the comings and goings between Orkney and Norway and England, and more than a note of pride in the achievement of building the great cathedral of St Magnus in Kirkwall. For the archaeologist, there are clues as to where to look for Norse farms and useful historical contexts for the runes in Maes Howe and the castle on Wyre. The sagas provide the backcloth for the visible monuments and exca-vated settlements, and the debris of everyday life recovered by excavation fills in some of the details.

Hogback tombstones and churches

The last chapter traced the development in Scotland of the fashion for hogback tombstones in the tenth and eleventh centuries. Hogbacks carved with roof-tiles and no other decoration continued in favour into the twelfth century in south-east Scotland and Orkney, barely dis-tinguishable from coped grave-covers, which were also carved with roof-tiles, other than by their curved ridge. Part of an eleventh-century hogback was found amongst builders' rubble

94 *Map of late Norse sites in the Northern Isles and Caithness mentioned in the text. 1 Sandwick; 2 The Biggings; 3 Mousa; 4 St Ninian's Isle; 5 Jarlshof; 6 St Boniface's Church; 7 Tuquoy; 8 St Magnus' Church; 9 Westness; 10 Brough of Birsay; 11 Cubbie Roo's Castle; 12 Ring of Brodgar; 13 Maes Howe; 14 Orphir; 15 Skaill; 16 Robertshaven; 17 Freswick.*

below the floor of the chancel of St Magnus' Cathedral in Orkney, and another came from the churchyard of St Olaf's Kirk, Kirkwall's church before the cathedral was built (Tankerness House Museum); both represent lay patrons at a time when, as *Orkneyinga Saga* records, Kirk-wall consisted of no more than a handful of houses. A fine late eleventh-century hogback is preserved within the church at Skaill in Deer-ness, Orkney, and provides a tangible link with the important Norse family estate which the original church here served; the Saga mentions Hlaupandanes in Sandwick as belonging in the mid-eleventh century to Thorkell, foster-father to Earl Thorfinn, and Skaill is the most likely location. Another eleventh-century monument is that from St Ninian's Isle in Shetland (now in Lerwick Museum); made of steatite from the outcrops on the adjacent mainland, this is a small and undecorated example with an excel-lent hogbacked profile.

The presence of a hogback tombstone should indicate late Norse burials, but it is otherwise difficult to point to graves of this period in churchyards which continued in use for several centuries. Even on the Brough of Birsay, Orkney, where slab-built graves are visible in the church-yard, unpublished excavations in the 1950s found two levels of graves neither of which can be securely dated; the church remained a place of pilgrimage and there could be late medieval burials here (95, 96). Two slab-lined graves were found in 1896 near St Peter's Church in Thurso, associated with a rune-inscribed cross (now in Thurso Museum); the graves contained an adult and a child, and the cross lay over the adult grave. The base of the cross is broken, and the incomplete inscription reads '. . . made this overlay after Ingolf his/her father'. The refer-ence to 'overlay' has been taken as evidence that this was not an upright cross but lay over the grave as a cover; this would be a most unusual situation for a cross, and the fact that the base is broken suggests that it stood in a socket in a recumbent slab and was subsequently snapped off, and thus the graves with which it was found

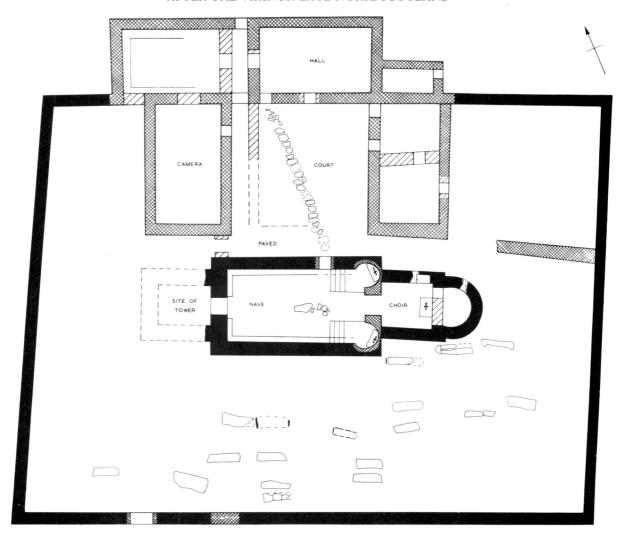

may not have been contemporary with the cross.

The ruins of a number of late Norse churches survive, from modest buildings such as Cille Donnain in South Uist to the splendid cathedral of St Magnus in Kirkwall. Most served secular communities, sometimes built close to the residences of important twelfth-century families such as St Mary's in Wyre, Orkney, near the castle of Kolbein Hruga, and Orphir on mainland Orkney where church and earl's residence

95 *Plan of the twelfth-century church and monastery on the Brough of Birsay, showing the upper level of graves in the churchyard.*

were close together. *Orkneyinga Saga* says of Orphir: 'in front of the hall, just a few paces down from it, stood a fine church' (chapter 66). Some served primarily ecclesiastical communities, such as the monastery on the island of

96 *The early twelfth-century church on the Brough of Birsay.*

Eynhallow between Rousay and mainland Orkney, or that at Strandibrough on Fetlar, Shetland. Two large churches in the Western Isles are thought to belong to this late Norse period: Carinish on North Uist and Eoropie on Lewis. The Brough of Deerness in Orkney has long been identified as a monastery, perhaps of Norse date: a stone-built chapel and a number of oblong foundations of houses lie on a precipitous rockstack, separated from the mainland but accessible on foot (97). This layout of church and houses is so similar to the Brough of Birsay that a secular status is as likely, if not more likely, than an ecclesiastical status for the site as a whole. Excavations of the chapel within its small enclosure revealed that the visible stone building had replaced an earlier timber and stone chapel, and that both are likely to be Norse in date.

The story of the murder of Earl Magnus Erlendsson on the island of Egilsay in about 1117 may imply that this fertile island had a monastery, and it was certainly one of the seats of the bishopric in Earl Rognvald's time, some twenty years later. The two earls, Magnus and Haakon

Paulsson, had joint control of Orkney but the relationship between them deteriorated. A meeting at the lawthing contrived, with the help of friends on both sides, to bring about a peace agreement; Haakon then suggested another meeting to confirm their goodwill on Egilsay during Holy Week (*Orkneyinga Saga*, chapter 47). The circumstances of this choice of location indicate a special sanctity about the island. Earl Magnus arrived first, only to see Haakon approaching with eight ships, clearly bent on treachery. Magnus spent the night in prayer in the church and was killed on Haakon's orders the following day. The church that survives today on Egilsay may be the one in which Magnus spent the night or it may have been built in his honour to replace an earlier and less splendid church – it has certainly been known ever since as St Magnus' church (**colour plate 9**).

The church consists of the normal rectangular

nave and square-ended chancel, but it is distinguished by the addition to the west end of a fine round tower, entered from the nave at ground level and from a first-floor gallery. The tower survives to a height of 15m (50ft) but originally its conical stone roof was probably at a height of some 20m (65ft). The design of this church belongs to a tradition shared round the North Sea, in eastern England in Norfolk and in northern Germany, with outliers in Sweden.

97 Aerial view of the Brough of Deerness; the chapel in its small enclosure has since been excavated and consolidated. Grass-covered foundations of rectangular buildings are also visible.

Church architecture is an aspect of twelfth-century Orcadian life in which the far-flung contacts of the earldom are particularly apparent. Another exotic church is St Nicholas at

Orphir, already mentioned as close to the earl's residence (**98**); the earl in question was Haakon Paulsson, who, after consolidating his position in Orkney following the murder of Earl Magnus, went on pilgrimage to Rome and Jerusalem 'where he visited the holy places and bathed in the river Jordan' (*Orkneyinga Saga*, chapter 52). One of the places that he would have visited in Jerusalem was the Church of the Holy Sepulchre, a round church which inspired the building of many round churches in Europe. The round church at Orphir and others that survive in Denmark reveal another architectural idea shared across the North Sea, but the coincidence of Earl Haakon's visit to Jerusalem is such that there is no need to seek an origin for the church in Scandinavia. It consists of a circular nave, 6m (20ft) in diameter, and a semicircular apse at the east side. Most of the nave was demolished when a new parish church (itself now demolished) was

98 *Aerial view of the round church at Orphir, with the remains of domestic buildings in the foreground.*

built in 1757, but early records describe its domed roof, and the apse is intact. A curious discovery is a runic inscription on a slab apparently from the fabric of the church (**99**), which reads 'the church is not good' – a message perhaps from someone who preferred more conventional architecture!

The most ambitious building project of the Norse earls was St Magnus' Cathedral in Kirkwall, as fine a minster as any in Scotland (**colour plate 10**). Building began in 1137 at the instigation of Earl Rognvald Kali Kolsson, nephew of St Magnus, and under the supervision of his father. It had been his father's suggestion that Rognvald should make a vow that, if he

99 *Runic inscription found in the wall of the later parish church at Orphir, which was built using stone from the twelfth-century round church.*

succeeded in gaining control of his earldom, he would 'build a stone minster at Kirkwall more magnificent than any in Orkney', dedicate it to St Magnus and 'provide it with all the funds it will need to flourish' (*Orkneyinga Saga*, chapter 68). The similarities between this great church and those at Dunfermline and Durham are such that it is believed that Rognvald must have enticed Anglo-Norman masons north to Kirkwall to build his minster in the most prestigious fashion of the day. The foundations were laid out for the entire building, and the choir was completed within a few years, but the whole cathedral was not finished until the fifteenth century, with the inevitable result that the original design was modified as time went on. Nevertheless, this splendid church has considerable integrity and visual impact, with its inspired use of alternate red and white stone; it conveys strongly the sense of having been the hub of Kirkwall life for more than eight centuries, and it belongs, literally, to the people of Kirkwall to this day.

The bishop of Orkney at the time building began was William the Old, whose episcopal seat was transferred from Birsay to Kirkwall and who would have been closely involved in the design of the new cathedral. He seems to have built himself a stone hall next to the cathedral, the foundations of which are incorporated into the Palace built by Bishop Reid in the mid-sixteenth century. The building that survives today consists of a large rectangular hall with a circular tower at its north-west corner. The masonry of the basal courses of the hall is clearly different from the masonry above: the courses

are more regular and the internal openings of the loopholes are built with alternate red and white freestones, both features echoing the early stonework of the cathedral. The surviving parts of the twelfth-century hall would have been the undercroft or ground floor of Bishop William's palace, the hall itself being on the first floor (**101**). It was in this building that the Norwegian King Haakon died on his way home after the Battle of Largs in 1263, and his body lay in state in the great hall before being buried in the cathedral – a temporary resting place until the spring when the weather allowed the King's body to be taken home to Bergen. A moving account of the King's last few days and his death is recorded in *Haakon Haakonsson's Saga*. Most probably it was also in this building that the Maid of Norway died in 1290, on her way at the age of seven years from Norway to Scotland to marry the Prince of Wales.

The Bishop's Palace would have been a comfortingly familiar building to the ailing King Haakon, for it was a smaller and simpler version of the great stone hall that he had built at Bergen, *Haakonshallen* (see **121**), finished only two years before his death. It had been a long and prosperous reign, during which his extensive kingdom had been in the mainstream of European culture; the Scottish earldom was part of a huge domain that included the Faeroes, Iceland

and Greenland as well as Norway itself (102). The Western Isles of Scotland had been formally ceded to Norway in 1098, after three centuries of Norse settlement, and the Battle of Largs was the result of persistent aggression by the Scots. The island of Bute was taken by the Scots sometime before 1200, and the great castle built by Walter Stewart at Rothesay (103) was twice captured for a short time by the Norsemen, first in 1230 and later by King Haakon in 1263.

Haakon left Bergen in early July 1263 and sailed with a great force across the North Sea first to Shetland and then to Orkney. It was an unhurried progress, for there were matters of state to attend to in both island groups, and the king celebrated the Norwegian festival of St Olaf's Day in Orkney on 29 July. Twelve days later, having failed to recruit the Orcadian force for which he had hoped, Haakon and the

100 St Magnus' Cathedral, Kirkwall; the warm tones of its red and white sandstone make this an unforgettable Romanesque minster.

Norwegian fleet left for the Western Isles. There they were joined by reinforcements both from the Isles and from the Isle of Man, and on their way south Haakon was able to send detachments to harass Kintyre and Bute. The main fleet sailed on to Lamlash Bay in Arran, and another detachment was sent to attack the island settlements in Loch Lomond. All these attempts to demoralize the Scottish king failed, and negotiations between Haakon and Alexander III came to nothing. By now it was late September, and the Firth of Clyde was lashed by storms. Several of Haakon's ships, including a richly laden cargo-ship, were blown aground on the main-

101 *Inside the Bishop's Palace, Kirkwall; the basement walls are thought to incorporate part of the original twelfth-century building.*

land at Largs, and both sides were intent upon salvage. The Battle of Largs was small-scale and neither king took part; to the Scots it was a victory, to the Norwegians an orderly retreat in which they burned their stranded ships and withdrew. Winter was now imminent, and Haakon returned northwards, collecting taxes on the way. The fleet arrived in Orkney on 29

October, and Haakon decided to remain there for the winter. His own illness intervened and he died on 16 December.

Haakon's efforts to assert his authority over

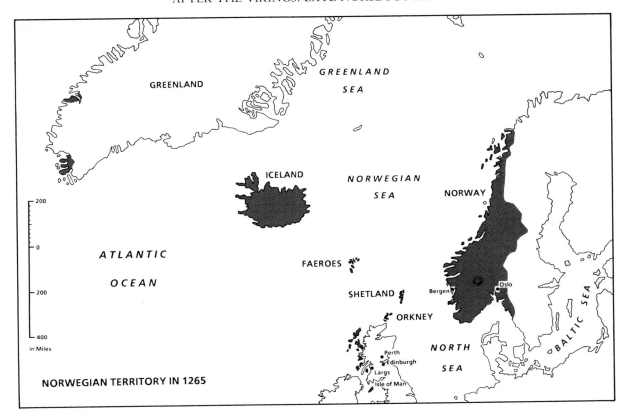

102 *Map showing the extent of Norwegian territory in 1265.*

the southern part of the earldom were thus ultimately unsuccessful, and the son who succeeded him, Magnus, was forced to recognize the futility of attempting to hold the Isles. By the Treaty of Perth in 1266, he relinquished both the Isle of Man and the Western Isles to the Scots.

Late Norse settlements

A number of the sites already described in earlier chapters continued in occupation into the twelfth and thirteenth centuries, including Jarlshof, the Brough of Birsay, Pool and the Udal. Others were founded at this period, although sometimes on sites with evidence of earlier but apparently not continuous occupation, as at Tuquoy on Westray. As always, the problem of sites excavated on the grounds of 'rescuing' them from coastal erosion is that part of the evidence has already been irrevocably lost and the sequence of building may well be incomplete.

Limited excavation at Tuquoy has confirmed its importance as a high-status late Norse farm on the site of a tenth-century settlement (see Chapter 3 for the environmental evidence from this earlier phase) and adjacent to the church of Crosskirk, probably of twelfth-century date. It has been argued that Tuquoy may have been the home of Thorkel Flettir and his family, who were prominent land-owners in Westray in the first half of the twelfth century (*Orkneyinga Saga*, chapters 65–73). Limited excavations in the 1980s uncovered part of a large rectangular hall with thick stone walls; incorporated into a secondary partition was a slab with a runic inscription reading 'Thorstein Einarsson carved these runes', using runes that indicate a twelfth-century date.

117

The settlement appears to have flourished until the fourteenth or fifteenth century. It lies at the very edge of the shore today, vulnerable to coastal erosion, and the excavations were designed to retrieve the maximum information with the minimum disturbance; the section along the low cliff was recorded, and only where necessary to explain the visible features did excavation extend a little way inland. But the severe January storms of 1993 washed away up to 3m (10ft) of the cliff, and the task of recording the new section was undertaken within weeks.

Many late Norse sites in the Northern Isles may be sealed beneath modern farms, for a successful farm is unlikely to be abandoned. Excavations at The Biggings on the Shetland island of Papa Stour will be very illuminating in this respect, because there occupation continued through the Middle Ages and down to the nineteenth century. The soil conditions, damp and peaty, have preserved not only a late Norse wooden floor (**104**) but wooden artefacts and pieces of woven cloth. Steatite vessels, spindle-whorls and baking plates are also prominent amongst the finds. Papa Stour is known from historical sources to have been part of the

103 *Rothesay Castle, Isle of Bute, was built in the thirteenth century and twice attacked successfully by Norsemen, first in 1230 and later by King Haakon IV of Norway in 1263.*

Shetland and Faeroes estate of Duke Haakon of Norway in the late twelfth century, and to have been the location of one of his houses.

Orkneyinga Saga makes it clear that Orphir was a place of considerable importance in the twelfth century, an earl's residence with an outstanding church. An account of the Christmas celebrations in 1135 includes a brief description of the earl's hall:

> There was a great drinking-hall at Orphir, with a door in the south wall near the eastern gable, and in front of the hall, just a few paces down from it, stood a fine church. On the left as you came into the hall was a large stone slab, with a lot of big ale vats on it, and opposite the door was the living-room. (chapter 66)

Brief though it is, this passage sketches quite a clear picture of the nucleus of the earl's estate. The drinking-hall was a spacious gabled building with its main door opposite the round

118

104 *Detail of the wooden floor at The Biggings, Papa Stour.*

walls uncovered by excavations many years ago, and some of these walls may well belong to Earl Paul's hall, but there are several phases of building within this complex and extensive new excavation is needed before they can be understood. Geophysical survey has indicated the presence of more walls to the east, which could be outhouses belonging to the twelfth-century estate or they could be earlier or later buildings. Recent excavations a little farther to the north have revealed not only a late Norse midden but beneath it the remains of a small corn-mill. The midden contained much food debris, including the bones of very large cod and saithe, and a tantalizingly incomplete runic inscription on a piece of cattle rib which reads 'this bone was in . . .'.

The corn-mill is a most important discovery, because it represents the earliest evidence of the type of horizontal mill that was common in Orkney and even more common in Shetland until recent times. This type of mill is known in Ireland from as early as the sixth century and was probably in use in Scotland in pre-Viking times and adopted by the Scandinavian settlers. All that survives at Orphir is the stone-lined subterranean chamber which housed the horizontal wheel, the head-race or lade, lined with upright slabs, which directed the water on to the wheel, and the tail-race which took the water away from the mill (see **107**). The tail-race here was built as an underground stone-walled channel roofed with stone slabs. The mill dates from sometime in the tenth or early eleventh century. Its presence underlines the substantial character of the Norse estate at Orphir even before the time of Earl Paul. Fieldwalking over a ploughed mound known as Lavacroon to the north-west of Orphir has produced evidence of industrial waste from iron and bronze working which is likely to be of Norse date.

Horizontal water-mills were common in Shetland into the twentieth century, and a restored example may be seen in the South Voe Croft Museum; there were fewer suitable watercourses in Orkney, but a nineteenth-century

church, aligned end-on to the prevailing wind and facing out to Orphir Bay and Scapa Flow. The private living-room was built on to the north wall of the hall, with its door opposite the main door, and there was probably a kitchen attached either to the north wall or to the east gable – the typical plan-form for a twelfth-century dwelling (**105**) but on a grand scale. The great wooden vats of ale, essential for feasting, stood on a stone slab close to the main door to keep the ale cool. The ale was to the left of the door and the benches and long hearth were beyond the vats.

Part of the church survives, but where is the great hall? Visible north of the church today are

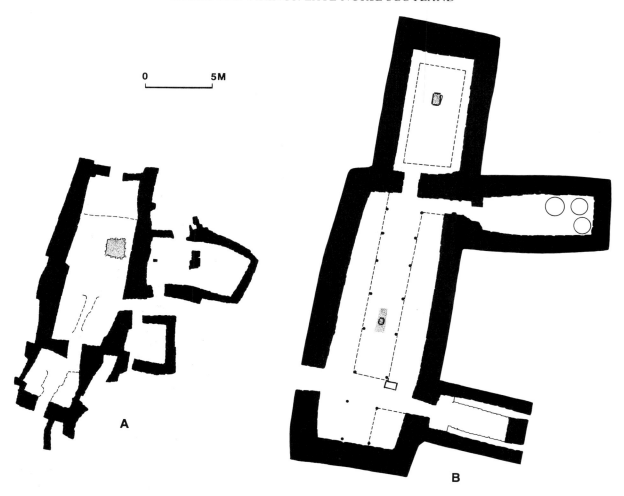

0   5M

A

B

105 *Plans of a twelfth-century farmhouse at Jarlshof (A) and an eleventh-century farmhouse at Stöng, Iceland (B), showing the development of extra rooms added on to the main living-hall. Stöng was the home of Gaukr Trandilsson, who is mentioned in one of the runic inscriptions in Maes Howe (pp.126–7).*

example survives near Dounby (**106**). Their local name is often 'click mill', from the noise made by the wooden revolving parts.

Norse castles

Fine residences were not the prerogative of earls. *Orkneyinga Saga* relates that 'a very able man' named Kolbein Hruga farmed on the island of Wyre in the mid-twelfth century and that 'he had a fine stone fort built there, a really solid stronghold' (chapter 84). It was so solid that almost a hundred years later it was described in *Haakon Haakonsson's Saga* as a difficult place to attack, and much of it survives today, known as Cubbie Roo's Castle (Kolbein's nickname would have been Kubbie and his surname has been reduced to Roo). It overlooks the sea passage between Wyre and Rousay which leads eastwards to Egilsay and westwards to mainland and Eynhallow Sound, and close by is the contemporary church of St Mary's (**108**). The adjacent modern farm bears the name Bu, suggesting that it may stand on the site of a high-status Norse farm. Strong though it must have

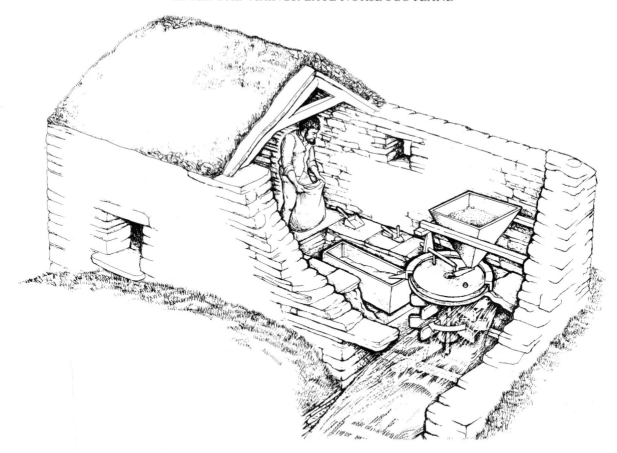

106 *An artist's reconstruction of the restored horizontal corn-mill at Dounby, Orkney, probably of early nineteenth-century date. The water flow turns the paddles of the horizontal wheel, which powers the mill machinery.*

been, the castle could not accommodate many people and Kolbein Hruga must have kept up his farm as well.

The idea of earthwork fortifications was familiar to the Norsemen, but this stone keep within its encircling defences may owe its design to the mottes of ultimately Norman origin which were being built in mainland Scotland at this time. The keep is about 8m (26ft) square with 2m (6½ft) thick walls, and it is surrounded at a distance of about 8m (26ft) by a stone wall with an outer ditch and bank; the keep survives to first-floor level, where the narrow projecting ledge that supported a timber floor may be seen and where the entrance once was. It is likely to have had at least two floors originally, in order to gain the height needed for a good view over the island and the adjacent seaways. The ground-floor chamber was probably used for storage and is furnished with a rock-cut tank.

Simply on the historical evidence of *Orkney-inga Saga*, this is one of the earliest castles in Scotland. The Castle of Old Wick on the Caithness coast was probably built in the twelfth century by Earl Harald Maddadson or one of his kinsmen; again this consists of a square stone keep. There are traces of similarly small and simple fortifications elsewhere in Orkney and Caithness which may also be of late Norse date, but they lack the historical support and cannot be dated securely on their architecture. The saga mentions 'strongholds' on the island of Damsay

107 *Norse horizontal mill at Orphir; in the foreground is the tail-race, draining from the lower chamber.*

Earl Thorfinn's escape with his wife from a hall set on fire by Earl Rognvald and his men.

Commercial deep-sea fishing?

More typical of the vast majority of late Norse farms are Jarlshof and Sandwick in Shetland, and Freswick in Caithness. The development of Jarlshof has already been discussed in Chapter 4; on the basis of a marked increase in the numbers of weights for fishing lines and nets, it was argued in the published report of Jarlshof that there had been a change in the economic life of the farm in the late Norse period in that fishing had become predominant. Relatively few fish-bones were recovered owing to the fact that systematic sieving of the midden deposits was not carried out, and it remained possible that the increase in discarded fishing equipment was the result of factors other than a growth in fishing itself.

Recent excavations at Sandwick and Freswick have, however, supported the theory of intensive fishing at this period; modern sieving and sampling techniques have recovered large quantities of fish as well as fishing equipment. At Sandwick most of the fish are under 500mm (20in) long, predominantly young saithe, but there are also bones of very large fish. At Freswick, the bones of three species were abundant: cod, saithe and ling, and their sizes suggested that two ranges were favoured, small fish under 200mm (8in) long and larger fish between 350mm (14in) and 900mm (35in) in length, although even larger fish up to 2m (6½ft) long are represented as well. Deep-sea line fishing on a large, perhaps even commercial, scale is implied by this evidence. Another late Norse midden at Robertshaven on the north coast of Caithness has yielded similarly large fishbones, and work is in progress analysing the material from both sites. Robertshaven has been interpreted as a seasonal site for processing fish and is dated to the eleventh or twelfth century on the basis of pottery and other artefacts – including a splendid bone pin, measuring

(chapter 66) and at Scrabster (chapter 111) and a 'fortress' at Cairston near Stromness (chapter 92), and the Norsemen were not above using a well-preserved broch when it suited them. Both *Orkneyinga Saga* and *Egil's Saga* mention two separate occasions when the great broch of Mousa in Shetland (**110**) was adopted as a refuge in the twelfth century. The great advantage of Kolbein Hruga's stone castle over conventional drinking-halls was that it was not vulnerable to the hit-and-run burnings by enemies that figure large in the Norse sagas – the appalling reality of which is explored by Dorothy Dunnett in her novel, *King Hereafter*, based on the *Orkneyinga Saga* account (chapter 28), dramatic in itself, of

230mm (9in) long and with a decorated head.

Freswick Bay was known to have been the location of a major late Norse farm from historical references in the sagas, and finds amongst the sand-dunes of pottery similar to pottery found at Jarlshof led to the identification of a settlement in 1937, the first Norse settlement discovered in mainland Scotland. At least eight buildings on two distinct stratigraphical levels were uncovered in several seasons of excavations, but more recent work on the site suggests that the building phases are more complex than first appeared. As well as fishbones, the middens have yielded evidence of oats and barley, and bones of cattle, sheep and pigs. A wide range of artefacts indicates that the main period of activity lay in the eleventh to thirteenth centuries; the range and quality of the finds and the extent of the known site suggests that this was a major settlement.

The late Norse farm at Sandwick lies on a

108 *An artist's reconstruction of the twelfth-century Norse castle known as Cubbie Roo's Castle, Wyre.*

sandy bay on the south-east coast of the Shetland island of Unst, and the outline of its walls is still visible although the excavation is finished. In the form in which it had survived the ravages of coastal erosion, it consisted of a true longhouse with accommodation for cattle at the lower end and an additional pair of rooms attached to one long wall; associated with it were enclosure walls. An interesting architectural feature was a 'cow-shaped' doorway: this led into the byre and consisted of an opening that was narrow at the base and widened above to allow for the breadth of the cow before narrowing a little towards the top. This neatly explains why some of the entrances into the byres at Jarlshof, where only the basal courses survive, seem improbably

109 *The ground-floor chamber of Cubbie Roo's Castle; access would have been by a wooden ladder from the first floor, and the central cistern supplied water.*

narrow. As well as the large quantities of fishbones mentioned already, the midden deposits yielded cattle and sheep, a few bones of pig, seal, horse and dog, and burnt grains of barley and oats. Large numbers of limpets and whelks were used either as food or fishbait. The artefacts showed trade contacts round the North Sea, with fragments of English and north German wheel-made pottery and bone combs from Norway. Another Norwegian import was an hourglass-shaped steatite lamp dating to the thirteenth or fourteenth century, a type found also at The Biggings on Papa Stour.

Runes

In common with other Germanic peoples, the Norsemen used an angular type of letter known as a rune, angular because it was developed as a means of cutting brief messages on wood or bone. Curving letters are perfectly suitable for writing in ink with a quill but very difficult to cut quickly with a knife. The runic alphabet was clearly derived in part from the Roman alphabet, because some runes are very similar to Roman letters although modified for easy cutting. Runes were in existence as early as the second century AD, but it is not known precisely where or when they were invented. They were used throughout Scandinavia and the Viking colonies for mess-

ages in the Old Norse language, some magical like the inscribed seal's tooth (see **38**) from the Brough of Birsay (Chapter 4), some commemorative like the inscribed cross from Thurso (see p.109), some informative and others purely for business purposes such as the wooden tally sticks found in Bergen. Runic inscriptions found in Scotland are confined to stone, bone and metal objects, but there must have been many cut on wood which have perished.

There are about 50 runic inscriptions surviving from Scotland, dating from the early Viking Age to the mid-thirteenth century and found mostly in the Western and Northern Isles. By far the largest collection can be seen on the walls of the great prehistoric tomb of Maes Howe in Orkney (**111** and **colour plate 11**), where some 30 inscriptions were carved on several occasions

110 The broch of Mousa, Shetland, still sufficiently impregnable to be used as a temporary refuge by Norsemen in the twelfth century.

when Norsemen broke into the mound in the twelfth century – one such occasion is recorded in *Orkneyinga Saga* (chapter 93) where the Norse name for Maes Howe is *Orkahaugr*. Earl Harald was on his way with his men from Stromness to Firth: 'During a snowstorm they took shelter in Orkahaugr and there two of them went insane, which slowed them down badly, so that by the time they reached Firth it was night-time.' The combination of a dank tomb and the wind howling in the darkness could well have been enough to tip a superstitious mind over the brink.

Two of the inscriptions mention crusaders having broken into the mound, while others write of beautiful women and treasure. One of the most interesting reads: 'these runes were carved by the man most skilled in runes in the western ocean with the axe which belonged to Gaukr Trandilsson in the south of Iceland' (112). By dint of some literary detective work, it has been discovered that the rune-carver was Thor-hallr Asgrimsson who was the great-great-great-grandson of Asgrimr Elliða-Grimsson, who, according to *Njal's Saga*, slew Gaukr Trandils-son. Gaukr's axe had stayed in his slayer's family for six generations, around 200 years, and was still in use – a vivid reminder of the problems for the archaeologist of using such objects as dating evidence. According to *Orkneyinga Saga*, Thor-hallr Asgrimsson captained the ship that brought

111 *Interior of the prehistoric chambered tomb of Maes Howe, Orkney; a small burial cell opens off each of three walls of the main chamber.*

Earl Rognvald and his fellow crusaders back to Orkney in 1153, thus explaining the Icelander's presence in Orkney if not in Maes Howe. Perhaps even then Maes Howe was high on the visitor's list of places to see.

Several of the Maes Howe inscriptions concern treasure: 'It is long ago that a great treasure was hidden here'; 'Happy is he who might find the great treasure'; 'Hakon alone bore the treasure out of this mound'; 'It is certain and true as I say, that the treasure has been moved from here. The treasure was taken away three

112 *Maes Howe; runic inscription to left of the cell in the south wall.*

nights before they broke into his mound'. Despite the insistence of these inscriptions, it is impossible that the original burials in this tomb, built some 4500 years ago, were accompanied by anything that the Norsemen would regard as treasure; the tomb belongs to pre-metalworking times and there can have been no silver or gold. Until excavations took place at Maes Howe in the 1970s, it was assumed that the treasure of the inscriptions was no more than wishful thinking. During the excavation, however, evidence was found for a rebuilding of the bank surrounding the mound (**114**), dated by radiocarbon analysis to the ninth century AD. Could it be that this prehistoric tomb was renovated and reused for a Viking warrior of the ninth century, buried with

his treasure alongside him? Was this the treasure that had become legendary by the twelfth century?

Maes Howe was not the only prehistoric monument to receive runic graffiti. A little to the north, the great stone circle known as the Ring of Brodgar must have been as baffling and powerful a sight to the Norsemen as it is to us today, and one twelfth-century visitor carved his name in runes, together with a small cross, on the inner face of one of the stones (it is a broken stump

today but may have been intact then) (**115**). These are cryptic tree runes but they can be read quite easily by counting the branches on either side of each rune and reading off the numbers on the following table, left-hand column first and then along the top.

	1	2	3	4	5	6
3	f	u	th	o	r	k
2	h	n	i	a	s	
1	t	b	m	l	y	

The pairs of numbers on each rune thus read 'biorn', the male name still common today, Bjorn.

113 *Maes Howe; runic inscription on the north-west buttress.*

114 *Aerial view of Maes Howe, showing the great mound covering the chamber and the encircling earthwork.*

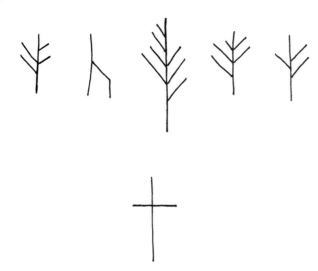

Somewhat misleading is the rune-stone in Princes Street Gardens in Edinburgh, beneath the Castle Esplanade. This is a typical Swedish commemorative stone with the inscription framed within a serpent-like design, and nothing resembling this stone was ever original to Scotland. It was in fact sent from Uppland in Sweden to Edinburgh in the eighteenth century by a wealthy Scots merchant interested in antiquities. The inscription reads: 'Ari set up the stone in memory of Hialm, his father. God help his soul.'

Simply because of the number of surviving monuments and the existence of *Orkneyinga Saga*, Orkney dominates every aspect of the late Norse period, but excavation elsewhere in Scotland may help to redress the balance in years to come.

115 *Runic inscription on a standing stone in the Ring of Brodgar, Orkney.*

CHAPTER EIGHT

Scotland's Viking inheritance

For many people, the quintessential remnant of Viking Scotland is the fire festival of Up-Helly-Aa, held in Lerwick on the last Tuesday in January. This is a genuine festival, dear to the hearts of Shetlanders, even if, in its present form, there is little that can be traced back beyond the nineteenth century. Preparations begin months in advance, for there are elaborate costumes to be sewn, hundreds of torches to be made from wood and sacking and a replica of a Viking longship to be built. On the night, a torchlight procession of guizers, men disguised in costume and masks, wends its way through the crowded streets, and the longship is dragged to the appointed spot where it is set on fire (**colour plate 12**). The rest of the night is spent in celebrations, with each of the fifty or so squads of guizers visiting in turn the various halls where people are gathered.

The festival grew out of the ancient Norse festival of Uphalliday on 29 January, which marked the end of the long midwinter celebrations. By the later nineteenth century, part of the celebrations consisted of blazing barrels of tar being dragged round the town by young men. At daybreak, the barrels were quenched and the youths donned fancy costumes, embarking on a round of friends' houses as guizers. The burning tar barrels were prohibited as too dangerous in 1874, and two years later the custom of a torchlight procession began; for the first time in 1881 this was held on the night of Up-Helly-Aa, and eight years later the idea of burning a replica

longship was introduced. The festival in its present form is thus little more than a hundred years old, but the name, the approximate date and probably the use of fire and disguise are ancient. Above all, this is a great communal enterprise which celebrates Shetland's Viking past.

The origins of Up-Helly-Aa had nothing to do with tourism, although it has certainly become an attraction for visitors over the last few decades. In contrast, the Largs Viking Festival was created in 1981 both to celebrate the Battle of Largs between the Scots and the Norsemen in 1263 and to encourage tourism – but its effect will again be to stimulate and satisfy interest in an important era of Scotland's past.

The octocentenary of St Magnus' Cathedral was celebrated in great style in Kirkwall over four days in 1937, beginning on St Olaf's Day, 29 July (a more convenient time of the year than St Magnus' Day on 16 April). Many dignitaries assembled from Orkney, Shetland, Scotland, Norway and Iceland to share the festivities with the people of Orkney, and a statue of St Olaf, the national saint of Norway, was presented to the Cathedral by the Bishop of Nidaros. Other gifts and addresses included 250 volumes of Norse literature gifted to Kirkwall by Norwegian publishers. A splendid pageant was performed by some 600 Orcadian players with the help of costumes and props loaned by the Norwegian National Theatre (**117–18**). The opening scene depicted Christian missionaries rescuing a girl

116 *Norse dragon carved on one of the buttresses inside the chamber of Maes Howe, Orkney.*

about to be sacrificed in the Stones of Stenness circle, and subsequent scenes enacted episodes in the history of the Norse earldom, ending with the consecration in 1151 of the new Cathedral by Bishop William. Among other events during this great celebration was a pilgrimage to St Magnus' Church in Egilsay with an open-air service in the churchyard, as well as services in the Cathedral itself on Sunday, 1 August.

The celebrations were a graphic reminder of the lasting bond between the Northern Isles and Norway, and it will be difficult in the future to emulate their enthusiasm and effort. To mark the 850th anniversary in 1987, a conference on St

Magnus Cathedral and the golden age of Orkney was held in Kirkwall, resulting in a fine volume of the conference papers by Scottish and Scandinavian scholars (*St Magnus' Cathedral and Orkney's Twelfth-Century Renaissance*, edited by Barbara Crawford, 1988). Will the tradition of celebrating the creation of this magnificent cathedral hold into the next millennium?

Shetland lacks any outstanding monument of the twelfth century, reflecting its distance from

the heart and wealth of the earldom. Yet Shetland remained Scandinavian in customs and language longer than Orkney, commonly using Norn, the descendant of the Old Norse tongue, as late as the eighteenth century (see below). Sir Walter Scott visited Shetland in 1814 with a party of Commissioners of the Northern Lighthouse Board. He wrote a journal, *Northern Lights*, and used his observations of the islands as a basis for his novel, *The Pirate*. Setting his story around the turn of the century, Scott wrote 'At this time, the old Norwegian sagas were much remembered, and often rehearsed, by the fishermen, who still preserved among themselves the ancient Norse tongue, which was the speech of their forefathers'.

The need for a tangible link with Shetland's Norse past was met in the early 1880s when Lerwick Town Hall was built; the main hall on the first floor is graced by a series of stained-glass windows commemorating historical figures from the Viking Age to the pledging of the islands to Scotland in 1469. Included among these figures were the Norwegian kings Olaf

117 *Pageant of 1937, in Kirkwall; Earl Magnus faces the treacherous Haakon.*

Tryggvason and Haakon Haakonsson, St Magnus and the Maid of Norway; this latter window was presented by the Royal Burgh of Kirkwall, in memory of the royal child who had died in Kirkwall almost 600 years before (**119**).

The Norn language survived as a spoken language into the eighteenth century in Shetland and Orkney, alongside Scots and Dutch, the latter being the result of longterm trade contacts. Scottish speech and culture had been gaining ground since the thirteenth century, when the earldom fell into Scottish hands, and were boosted in the later fifteenth century when the islands became part of Scotland. Nevertheless, the strength of the Norn language, particularly amongst fishermen, was such that many Norse words continued in use long after the language as a whole had ceased; dictionaries compiled in the early twentieth century recorded some 10,000

118 *Pageant of 1937, in Kirkwall; Earl Rognvald vows to build a minster.*

Norn words in use in Shetland and about 3000 in Orkney. Alongside language, the Norse custom of using patronymics rather than true surnames survived into the seventeenth century, again surviving longer in Shetland than in Orkney. As in modern Iceland, people were given a Christian name and were known as the daughter or son of their father: for example, Garto Paulis douchter (daughter of Paul) or Nichole Johnsoun (son of John), just as an Icelander of today might be named Gudrun Bjornsdottir (daughter of Bjorn).

The practical links between the Northern Isles and Norway were equally lasting, for Orkney and Shetland needed Norway's timber and Norway needed Orkney's grain. Ready-dressed wood for boats and houses – kits, almost, in the modern sense – were still being imported into the Northern Isles in the sixteenth and seventeenth centuries. Ethnological studies have demonstrated that the links between northern and western Scotland and the Faeroes and Iceland remained as strong as those between Scotland and Norway; the types and names of various farming implements and practices can be

shown to be closely related.

If the archaeology of the Northern Isles has seemed to dominate this book, it is a legitimate reflection of the state of our knowledge of Viking Age and late Norse Scotland. It is also a reflection of the degree to which Orkney and Shetland were influenced by a long period of Scandinavian dominance.

The predecessor of St Magnus' Cathedral in Kirkwall was the church of St Olaf, which no longer survives apart from a single ornate doorway, sadly weathered, now set into a wall in St Olaf's Wynd (**120**). The minister of St Olaf's at the end of the nineteenth century was the Reverend J.B. Craven, who published his well-researched *History of the Church in Orkney* in 1901. He wrote 'We are far too much inclined to look upon ancient peoples as total savages'. Elsewhere the Vikings have been portrayed as

unthinking and uncivilized barbarians, taking and not giving. The aim of the present book has been to draw attention to the wealth of monuments and artefacts bequeathed to us by the Vikings in Scotland, and to the lasting influence of that people who, noted at times for slaughter and bloodshed, turned out to be not entirely savage.

120 *The doorway from St Olaf's Church, Kirkwall, now built into a wall in St Olaf's Wynd.*

121 *Haakon's Hall in Bergen, Norway, is a grander version of the Bishop's Palace in Kirkwall.*

119 *Stained-glass window in Lerwick Town Hall, depicting the Maid of Norway.*

Monuments and
museums to visit

Sites in the care of Historic Scotland are open to the public, but those not in State care lie on privately-owned land and permission to visit *must* be sought from the landowner. The major collection of Viking artefacts is in the Royal Museum of Scotland, Queen Street, Edinburgh, but several local museums have good displays.

Shetland

Cunningsburgh (NGR HU 423270)
Outcrops of steatite (soapstone) on either side of the Catpund Burn bear clear traces of prehistoric and Norse quarrying (see p.62) (privately owned, see above).

Jarlshof, Sumburgh (NGR HU 398095)
Extensive and well preserved remains of a Norse settlement (see pp.62–71, 120 and 122–3); small museum (Historic Scotland). There are plans to reconstruct one of the Norse houses nearby.

Law Ting Holm, Tingwall (NGR HU 418434)
At the northern end of the Loch of Tingwall, a boggy promontory extends into the loch. This was once a small island connected to the shore by a narrow causeway, and the Norse lawthing was held on the island (see p.71). The causeway can still be seen (privately owned, see above).

Underhoull, Unst (NGR HP 573043)
The remains of an excavated Norse house lie on the slope to the north of the small sandy bay of Lunda Wick on the west coast of the island of Unst (see pp.71–2) (privately owned, see above).

Shetland Museum, Lower Hillhead, Lerwick
Displays include Norse artefacts from Jarlshof and the hogback from St Ninian's Isle.

South Voe Croft Museum, South Mainland (NGR HY 398146)
The croft buildings include a horizontal mill in working order (see p.119).

Orkney

Brough of Birsay, Mainland (NGR HY 239285)
Well preserved Norse houses, church and monastery (see pp.52–7, 110–11 and **colour plate** 3); the Brough is a tidal island and access depends upon low tide (Historic Scotland).

Brough of Deerness, Mainland (NGR HY 596087)
Norse chapel set within a small enclosure on a precipitous rock-stack on the east coast (see p.111); also rectangular house foundations, but these have not been excavated (Orkney Islands Council).

Bishop's Palace, Kirkwall (NGR HY 449108)
Kirkwall's oldest secular building; most of the Palace dates from the sixteenth century but the basal courses of the main block are thought to date from the thirteenth century (see p.114–16) (Historic Scotland).

Cubbie Roo's Castle, Wyre (NGR HY 441262)
Twelfth-century Norse castle preserved to first-floor level; St Mary's Chapel nearby was the contemporary church (see pp.120–4) (Historic Scotland).

Dounby Click Mill, Mainland (NGR HY 325228)
An early nineteenth-century example of a horizontal mill, restored to working order (see p.121) (Historic Scotland).

Gurness, Mainland (NGR HY 381268)
Prehistoric broch and settlement, Pictish house (see pp.23–5), visitor centre (Historic Scotland). The grave-goods from the Viking burial are in Tankerness House Museum.

Maes Howe, Mainland (NGR HY 318127)
Prehistoric chambered tomb with many inscriptions in Norse runes carved inside the burial chamber (see pp.125–8, 131, **colour plate 11**) (Historic Scotland).

Orphir, Mainland (NGR HY 334044)
Remains of twelfth-century round church and earl's residence (Historic Scotland); basal remains of Norse horizontal mill (see pp.110, 113, 118–19, 122).

Ring of Brodgar, Mainland (NGR HY 294133)
Prehistoric stone circle with Norse runes (see p.129) carved on the inner side of one of the broken stones (third stone to the north side of the entrance) (Historic Scotland).

St Boniface's Church, Papa Westray
(NGR HY 488527)
Twelfth-century church with a late hogback tombstone in the churchyard (see p.109); this hogback may be in its original position and has a small headstone.

St Magnus' Cathedral, Kirkwall (NGR HY 449108)
Intact Romanesque cathedral in use today; building began in 1137 to commemorate the murdered Earl Magnus (see pp.113–15, **colour plate 10**).

St Magnus' Church, Egilsay (NGR HY 466303)
Well-preserved twelfth-century church with a round tower (see pp.111–12, **colour plate 9**) (Historic Scotland).

Skaill, Deerness, Mainland (NGR HY 588063)
Well-preserved hogback tombstone inside the Session House alongside the modern church (see p.109). The site of the Norse settlement lies between Skaill farm and the shore, but the buildings are no longer visible (privately owned, see above).

Tankerness House Museum, Broad Street, Kirkwall
Pictish and Viking galleries display finds from the Brough of Birsay, Gurness, Skaill, Point of Buckquoy and elsewhere. In the courtyard there is a modern Norwegian boat known as an oselvar, which is a small fishing boat very close in design to the Viking boats discovered in burials at Westness and Scar.

Caithness
Castle of Old Wick, Wick (NGR ND 369489)
A ruined tower thought to be a Norse castle of twelfth- or early thirteenth-century date (see p.121) (Historic Scotland).

St Mary's Church, Crosskirk (NGR ND 024700)
Twelfth-century church.

Thurso Heritage Museum, High Street, Thurso
Display includes rune-inscribed Norse cross (see pp.109–10).

Southern and eastern Scotland
Abercorn Kirk, West Lothian (NGR NT 081791)
In a room off the vestry of this fine sixteenth-century church are two hogback tombstones and fragments of a third, dating to the eleventh and twelfth centuries.

Brechin Cathedral, Brechin, Angus
(NGR NO 596601)
The earliest parts of the cathedral are of thirteenth-century date, but the existence of an earlier monastery is implied by an eleventh-century round tower (Historic Scotland), an elaborately carved hogback tombstone of the early eleventh century (see p.98) and a Pictish cross-slab, both of which are displayed within the cathedral.

Govan, Glasgow (NGR NS 553 658)
Within the Old Parish Church lie five hogback tombstones of tenth-century date (see p.97).

Inchcolm Abbey, Isle of Inchcolm, Firth of Forth
(NGR NT 189826)
On a knoll to the west of the medieval monastery, there is a tenth-century hogback tombstone (see p.98 **colour plate 8**) (Historic Scotland).

Whithorn, Galloway (NGR NX 444403)
The thirteenth-century priory church incorporates some older building (see p.99–101) (Historic Scotland). The visitor centre includes a museum, to which new exhibits from the recent excavations are constantly added, and an excellent video about the history of Whithorn and about the excavations by the Whithorn Trust.

Hunterian Museum, University of Glasgow
Displays include the bronze balance from Gigha (see p.84).

Meigle Museum, Perthshire
Large collection of Pictish and later sculpture, including a hogback tombstone (see p.98) (Historic Scotland).

Nithsdale District Museum, Church Street, Dumfries
Extensive collection of early Christian and later sculpture, including two hogback tombstones.

St Andrews, Cathedral Museum, Fife
Extensive collection of sculpture includes a hogback

tombstone formerly in St Leonard's School (Historic Scotland).

St Vigeans Museum, near Arbroath, Angus
Large collection of Pictish and later sculpture (p.98) (Historic Scotland).

Stewartry Museum, St Mary Street, Kirkcudbright
Displays include a Viking sword and other finds from St Cuthbert's Churchyard, and a handled linen smoother from Gribdae Farm.

Argyll

Iona

A good stretch of the earthwork surrounding the early monastery survives to the north-west of the medieval abbey. Eighth-century high crosses; Norse sculpture in the Abbey Museum (see pp.19–20, 91).

Further reading

Bailey, Richard N. *Viking Age Sculpture*, Collins, London, 1980.

Baldwin, John R. *Caithness: a cultural crossroads*, Scottish Society for Northern Studies and Edina Press Ltd, Edinburgh, 1982.

Beck, Robert *Scotland's Native Horse: its history, breeding and survival*, G.C. Book Publishers, Wigtown, 1992.

Crawford, Barbara E. *Scandinavian Scotland*, Leicester University Press, Leicester, 1987.

Donaldson, Gordon *A Northern Commonwealth: Scotland and Norway*, Saltire Society, Edinburgh, 1990.

Duncan, Archibald A.M. *The Making of the Kingdom*, Mercat Press, Edinburgh, 1975.

Farrell, R.T. (ed.) *The Vikings*, Phillimore, 1982.

Fenton, Alexander and Palsson, Hermann (eds) *The Northern and Western Isles in the Viking World: survival, continuity and change*, John Donald Publishers, Edinburgh, 1984.

Foote, Peter and Wilson, David M. *The Viking Achievement*, Sidgwick and Jackson, London, 1970.

Graham-Campbell, James *The Viking World*, New Haven, New York, 1980.

Graham-Campbell, James and Kydd, Dafydd *The Vikings*, British Museum Publications, London, 1980.

Hunter, J.R. *Rescue Excavations on the Brough of Birsay 1974–1982*, Society of Antiquaries of Scotland Monograph Number 4, Edinburgh, 1986.

Loyn, Henry R. *The Vikings in Britain*, Batsford, London, 1977.

Morris, Christopher D. and Rackham, D. James *Norse and later settlement and subsistence in the north Atlantic*, Glasgow University Department of Archaeology, Occasional Paper no 1, Glasgow, 1992.

Oram, Richard D. and Stell, Geoffrey P. *Galloway: Land and Lordship*, Scottish Society for Northern Studies, Edinburgh, 1991.

Palsson, Hermann and Edwards, Paul *Orkneyinga Saga*, The Hogarth Press, London, 1978.

Renfrew, Colin (ed.) *The Prehistory of Orkney BC 4000–1000 AD*, Edinburgh University Press, Edinburgh, 1985.

Richards, Julian D. *Viking Age England*, English Heritage/Batsford, London, 1991.

Ritchie, Anna and Breeze, David J. *Invaders of Scotland*, HMSO, Edinburgh, 1991.

Royal Commission on the Ancient and Historical Monuments of Scotland *Argyll: An Inventory of the Monuments, vol 4, Iona*, HMSO, Edinburgh, 1982.

Smith, Brian (ed.) *Shetland Archaeology*, The Shetland Times Ltd, Lerwick, 1985.

Smyth, Alfred P. *Warlords and Holy Men: Scotland AD 80–1000*, Edinburgh University Press, Edinburgh, 1984.

Thomson, William P.L. *History of Orkney*, Mercat Press, Edinburgh, 1987.

Glossary

baking plate A thin disc of steatite which was used as a griddle for baking on the open hearth.

cist A pit lined and often covered with stone slabs; used for storage or for burials.

clinker-built Made with overlapping planks of wood; normally used of boats.

cross-slab A slab of stone carved with a cross.

kerbed cairn A cairn of stones, usually covering a burial, with a kerb of low upright stones.

line-sinker A stone weight for fishing-lines.

loomweight A stone weight for keeping taut the vertical threads on an upright hand-loom.

midden A domestic rubbish heap.

ring-money A plain penannular silver armlet used as bullion in place of coins.

ring-pin A long dress-pin, usually made of bronze, with a ring through its head; a thread attached to the ring could be wound round the tip of the pin when in place to prevent it slipping out of the garment.

sneck A door-latch usually made of wood or whalebone.

spindle-whorl A circular weight, usually made of stone, with a central perforation to take the wooden spindle; used to spin fibres into thread.

spiral-ring A finger-ring of bronze, silver or gold, made by twisting a thin rod into a spiral.

steatite A soft stone or talc, also known as soapstone, which is easy to carve.

strap-end A metal fitting, often U-shaped, which strengthened the end of a leather strap or belt.

wall-head The top of the wall; in the case of a house, the roof-timbers rested on the wall-head.

wet sieving A technique for retrieving organic material and very small objects from excavated soil; the soil is placed in wire baskets of a fine mesh and water is passed through it, washing away the soil and leaving charcoal, burnt grain, fishbones, beads etc.

whetstone A stone on which metal blades can be sharpened.

Index